"Nobody wishes more than I do to see such proofs as you exhibit, that nature has given to our Black brethren, talents equal to those of other colours of man — and that the appearance of a want of them is owing merely to the degraded condition of their existence both in Africa and America..."

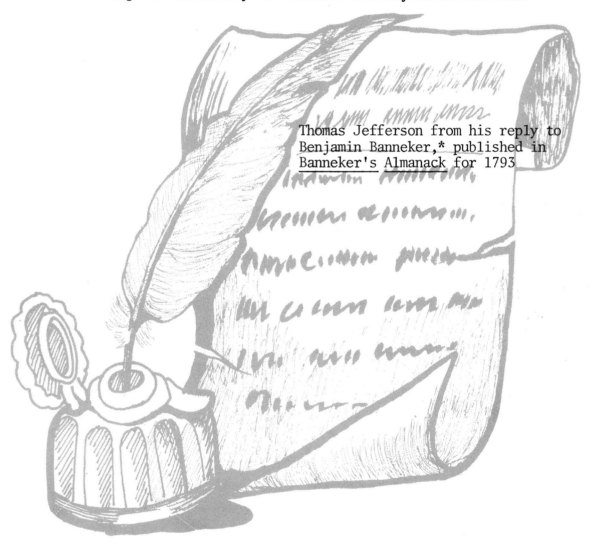

Thomas Jefferson from his reply to Benjamin Banneker,* published in Banneker's Almanack for 1793

*Benjamin Banneker was a brilliant Black mathematician and one of the three commissioners appointed by George Washington to *plan the city of Washington, D.C.* He and G. Ellicott chose the sites for the White House, the Capitol, and many other buildings. Banneker also invented the first clock constructible from American parts, was an astronomer, and for decades published an Almanac & Ephemeris. For additional information, see *Black Scientists of America,* National Book Company, 1990.

Black Inventors
of
America

McKinley Burt, Jr.

National Book Company
Portland, Oregon

0-89420-095-X

296959

Contents

Preface   7

The Romance of the Rails

    Prologue   19

    Andrew J. Beard (Railway Coupling)   22

    Granville T. Woods (Air Brake, Electric Railroad, etc.)   28

    Richard B. Spikes (Semaphore, Automatic Gear Shift)   44

    Others   52

Creators of Industry and Jobs

    Prologue   53

    Jan Matzeliger (Shoe Last Machine)   56

    Norman Rillieux (Sugar Refiner)   80

    Frederick M. Jones (Truck and Rail Refrigeration, etc.)   92

    Elijah M. McCoy (Lubricating Valves)   106

Black Capitalism

    Invention and Innovation as a vital new American Force   121

    Statistics in Ebony   131

Appendix

    The Unfinished Declaration of Independence of the United States   139

    The Patent Process: Economic and Social Factors   140

    Patent and Invention Index   141

    Bibliography and Suggested Readings   149

Preface

THE GENERAL, 1855

The tremendous influence of the Black Inventor upon American Industry and Culture is a force which is still structuring our society. In a decision as recent as May, 1969, the United States Supreme Court once again underscored the viability of the contribution. This case, cited below, has such obvious relevance (and lends such vigorous support to positive evaluations of Black Genius) that I am reminded of that familiar quotation: "Thou shalt not bear false witness against thy neighbor." It is an accepted fact that we are influenced, guided, and motivated by our Communications. For so many scholars, historians, and our culture-in-general to have deleted the magnificent accomplishments of an entire race . . . is to collectively " . . . Bear False Witness."

Fortunately, many of these "sins of omission" are being rectified at last. In 1962, the American Historical Association, along with two similar groups in England — The British Association for American Studies and The Historical Association of England and Wales — began an International Research Project entitled, "National Bias in the School Books of the United Kingdom and the United States."

The "Automatic Railcar Coupler" was the focal point of the Federal Safety Appliance Act, which Congress enacted at the turn of the century. Andrew J. Beard, a black laborer in an Alabama freight yard, invented and patented this device in 1897 (US #594,059). This act made it unlawful for a railroad to supply cars which did not couple automatically on impact. So important was this invention to the development of America's huge railroad complexes (which supported a burgeoning, industrial society) that, in 1908, Congress took an additional step by passing the Federal Employer's Liability Act. This legislation gave railroad employees the right to sue in Federal Court when injured as a result of equipment failure — should such failure be a violation of the original Safety Appliance Act.

The specific case, cited this year, arose from injuries sustained by a workman in Iowa while helping load and move freight cars. The victim of the accident sued the railroad company, claiming that his injury resulted from a defective *coupler* and that this defect violated the Appliance Act. The case was decided against the plaintiff as he "was the employee of the Grain Elevator Company, not of the *railroad*."

This case revealed, however, in detail, the entire social, economic, and legal pyramid which has evolved from the compassion-inspired invention of a Southern black laborer. It might be well to point out that subsequent and similar legislation involving the safety and welfare of workers in mines, factories, building trades, and other fields, drew its form and substance from this pioneering concept of invention and human concern. Throughout the Industrial Nations of the world, we find similar legislation based upon this American model.

The element of *motivation*, in relationship to achievement, cannot be over-emphasized! The author is able to recall, from his own black youth, the drive and determination to fully participate in the American Scene; enlightened and inspired by the knowledge that so much of America's Scene was 'His Scene.' It was not an alien world of which he wanted no part — or that was rejected because it seemed to have no blackness, no soul! — but rather he was led to perceive just how much of the world bears the stamp of an Ebony Psyche — the thousands of inventions and innovations of America's blacks. For him there could no longer be borne "False Witness!"

The first patent known to have been granted to a black was for a corn planting machine. This was issued to Henry Blair, of Maryland, on October 14, 1934. Two years later, he was granted a second patent, for a similar device involving the planting of cotton. Blair was one of the more fortunate slaves, who was able to have his freedom purchased; a slave, of course, could not file a patent in his own name.

It seems probably that there were a considerable number of such inventions, since the Confederacy found it necessary to include a section in its constitution, stating that "The Owner of a Slave Also Controlled His Inventions."

During this same era, black inventors were responsible for important strides in New England's ship-building and fishing industries. In 1848, Lewis Temple, born in Richmond, Virginia, had settled in New Bedford, Massachusetts, where he worked as a metalsmith. He invented the "Toggle Harpoon," which so improved whaling

By 1865:

". . . Almost half the number of seamen in America were black."

". . . Four black sailors had won the Congressional Medal of Honor: Robert Black, USS Marblehead; John Lawson, USS Hartford; James Mifflin, USS Brookland; and Joachim Pease, USS Kearsage."

". . . Lewis Temple had invented the toggle-harpoon and doubled the whaling catch of New England; James Forten, of Philadelphia, invented the 'Forten Sail Control;' and built a sail factory employing approximately fifty workers, both black and white."

methods in the nineteenth century that the average catch was *doubled*. It soon became the standard harpoon for the world's whaling industry.

Robert Lewis, of Maine, was another black inventor of devices for the fishing fleets of his day. James Forten of Philadelphia invented a mechanism that helped in the control of sails. He became wealthy; and the U.S. Navy veteran built a sail factory employing fifty workers, both black and white.

Not so astute was a black inventor from Texas, one Henry Sigler of Galveston, who patented "an Improved Fishhook" in 1854 and sold it for $650. Texas inventors soon caught on, however, and are well and profitably represented in this book's Black Patent Index.

It might be well to consider here the historical situation: the "backlighting" for our creative stage. The accomplishments of the earliest of the black inventors become almost incomprehensible when the mind is forced to consider the harshness of the scene. Seven out of eight slaves worked on the Southern plantations, from early sunrise to late sunset. They were considered merely another form of property or chattel. The owner of his overseers set the working conditions and served as both judge and jury over the slaves. Those that worked as house servants were treated somewhat better than the field slaves.

At sea, however, black man could enjoy an equality denied him on land and almost half of the number of seamen in America were black. In the Southern ports, the "free" black seamen were seen as a threat to the slave system and, therefore, were confined to jail until their ships were due to sail.

The abolition of slavery also abolished the incentive-stifling plantation system, making way for the new Industrial Capitalism. It was also the age of a second "Renaissance," one of invention, perception, and innovation. This time, however, the catalyst-bearing Moors did not come directly from Africa; but, between 1871 and 1899, some 195 black American inventors were granted patents. Many proffered a wide array of inspired devices, with over half being generic or basic.

By 1900, Henry E. Baker, Assistant Examiner of the United States Patent Office, was able to publish "Four Giant Volumes on Black Inventors." By 1913 his list of "Black Contributions to American Science and Industry" numbered over a thousand.

Today most of this material may be examined at Howard University, where it will be found in the "Moorland Collection of Black Patents."

The author is deeply indebted to Dr. Helen Edmonds, Dean of the Graduate School at North Carolina Central University, in Durham. It was with the help of this world-recognized authority on black history, that the author was able to locate previously inaccessible material. Dr. Edmonds, a very competent lecturer and thorough researcher, further assisted the author's efforts to confirm background material when she conducted a two-week seminar on "The Negro in American History" during 1969.

To understand how so many blacks, supposedly one step from savagery, could produce so much, so soon, and of such a sophisticated nature, we must turn to another authority. Dr. Robert I. Rothberg of Harvard clarifies much of the "mystery." In his authoritative "Political History of Tropical Africa," Professor Rothberg (like Life Magazine, in its series on Black History) makes it very plain: That we may no longer assume that the 15th century European found an African living in barbarism and slavery. Much of the factual material was omitted from American texts . . .to protect the conscience of those who had built their economic citadels upon the traffic in slavery. Until now, there has been a wall of silence concerning the African Civil Service, postal systems, iron workers, armorers, ship builders, universities, astronomers, mathematicians, etc.

Also, there can be no more accurate or complete record than the official journals of the United States' military or the U.S. Congressional Record. Even the most adamant of slavers stopped short of tampering with these. Now, we may see and understand the volatile context from which the black inventor rose: a strange and soul-testing furnace, balanced against an inspired talent which would not be denied. Consequently, it is not too surprising to find these records in frequent reference to an oft-denied literacy and social conscience among the black slaves.

General Saxton, Commander of the United States Department of the South, writes: "On some of these islands (off the coasts of Georgia and South Carolina), the freedmen have established Civil Governments with Constitutions and Laws. Further, they have set up all the different Departments for Schools, Churches, Building Roads, and Other Improvements."

Almost half of the black, reconstruction-period Congressmen were "College Educated." The Congressional Record for this period reflects an interest in, and an intellectual grasp of, a wide range of subjects, in addition to Civil Rights, including Tariff Legislation (to support the surge of industrial growth and innovation), a pension plan for soldiers, Federal aid to education, and much other "modern" legislation.

Senator Blanche K. Bruce, of Mississippi, fought for fair and equitable treatment for the Indian and against Chinese Exclusion Laws. An ex-slave, Senator Bruce finally gained an education in Missouri and at Oberlin College. He returned to Mississippi a free man, becoming in turn a prosperous planter, school teacher, sheriff, and, in 1871, Assessor of Taxes for Bolivar County.

As the most active member of the Board of Levee Commissioners, he pioneered many novel approaches to the "Improvement of Navigation." His overall dedication to the growth and development of his state, and to all of its citizens, black and white, brought him to the attention of President Garfield, who appointed him Registrar of the United States Treasury Department. In 1889 he was appointed U.S. Recorder of Deeds. This dedicated black administrator and economic innovator died in 1898 after 28 years of exemplary public service. And he was but one of many.

"To read or write Negro History is now no longer to venture into Terra Incognito," said Dr. Benjamin Quarles of Morgan State College, Baltimore. Professor Quarles, in an article in the *Saturday Review* (September 3, 1966), emphasized, from his vantage point as an accomplished historian, that scholars must recognize the contribution of the black as being essential to the understanding of our country's past. The author was willing to go further and say that many of today's traumatic social adjustments could have been avoided . . . had our historians performed their scientific tasks with the same uncompromising dedication as did their scholarly opposites in the physical sciences!

The author is fortunate in that *his* own innovations and inventions have had the exposure of modern communications: television, newspapers, etc. In this day and time, the public cannot help but be aware . . . and it is therefor more difficult for those who are motivated by various insecurities of race or status to obstruct, in turn, the motivation and inspiration of on-coming youth. It is to these young, with whom he finds no difficulty in communicating, that the author dedicates this book — That more blacks shall "know their fathers" . . . and that more children and adults, of all races, shall know a rare breed of Great Americans.

Man and His Machines

It would be to our advantage, in considering the scope and application of the works of these Black Inventors, if we were to briefly review what a "machine" is all about! This will greatly enhance our perspective when we encounter descriptive data from the Patent Recording.

The following are some examples:

Richard B. Spikes, in his patent on the Automatic Gear Shift, devised a system for operating "from the driver's compartment of a motor vehicle through a selective indicator, and arranged for automatically shifting the gears and transmission selected upon disengaging the conventional clutch."

Jan Matzeliger announced that he had invented an Automatic Shoe Last Machine, that would make economy-priced shoes available to all peoples of the world. "Figure 16 is a plan view of the channel for carrying the tacks to the driver and its connections."

Granville T. Woods, who put railroading into a modern idiom with the "Third Rail," the Air Brake, Induction Telegraphy, ad infinitum, petitioned the Commissioner of Patents, "there is one contact-maker used for conveying current to the switch magnets only, and one other contact-maker for conveying current to the car motor only." Only six mechanical functions apply!

Basically, there are six "simple" machines — meaning that all of the mechanical devices used by man must fall under one or more of these classifications. A "simple" machine is defined as "a simple device (lever, pulley, inclined plane, etc.) that alters the magnitude or direction, or both, of an applied force." On the following page is an illustrated list of the six simple machines.

A "compound" machine, then, is a combination or system of simple machines. Familiar devices which involve combinations of simple machines are compound

The Six Simple Machines

1. Wheel

2. Pulley

3. Lever

4. Wedge

5. Inclined Plane

6. Screw

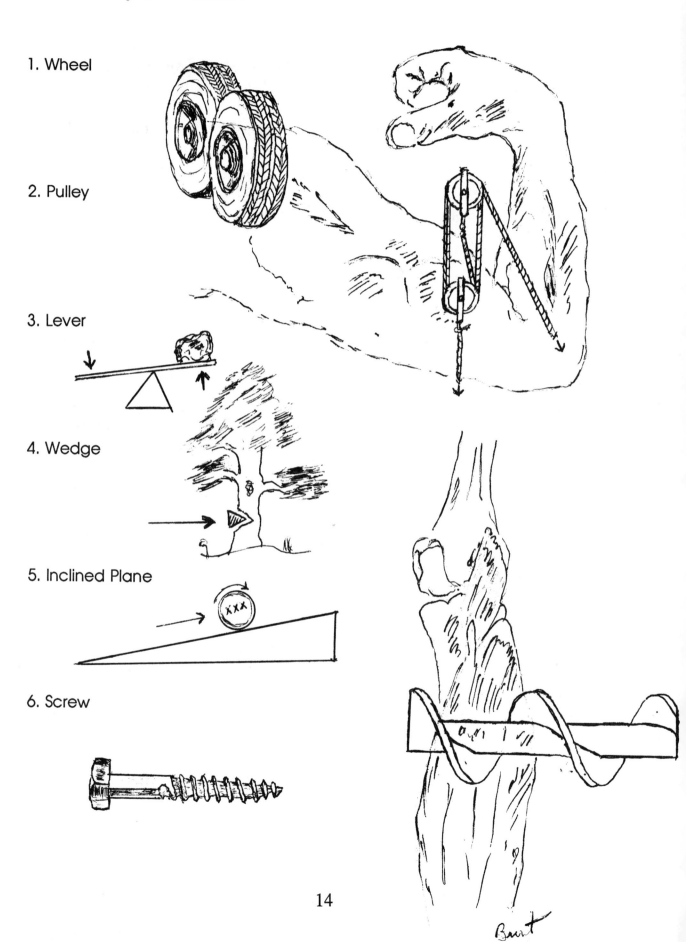

14

machines such as the automobile engine, lawnmower, movie projector, typewriter, and the human body . . . with its combinations of muscles, tendons, and ligaments.

See if you can properly classify the following devices as being either a "simple" or a "compound" machine:

can opener	Yo-Yo
crowbar	escalator
pencil sharpener	scissors
swing	automobile jack

Now, let us take a closer look at machines. Often we define a machine as a combination of parts useful for the transmission of energy and/or motion. *Energy* is thought of as "the ability to do work." Energy may be in the "potential" form — that is, stored — in the form of a compressed spring, water behind a dam, coal, gasoline. Then, we may find energy in its "kinetic" form, such as a *moving* spring, or a moving car. Other examples of this *release* of potential are electricity, heat, light, (from burning coal or gas), and atomic energy.

The fundamental principle of all machines is the *obtaining of a mechanical advantage* (see illustration of the lever). Mathematically, this is "the Ratio of Resistance or Load to Applied Force." *Prime Movers* are machines which convert sources of potential energy into mechanical power, such as gasoline engines, turbines, jet engines, windmills, etc.

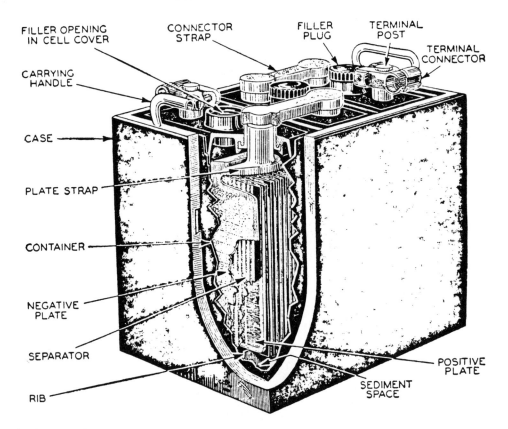

A. **Potential Energy** -- Electric Storage Battery

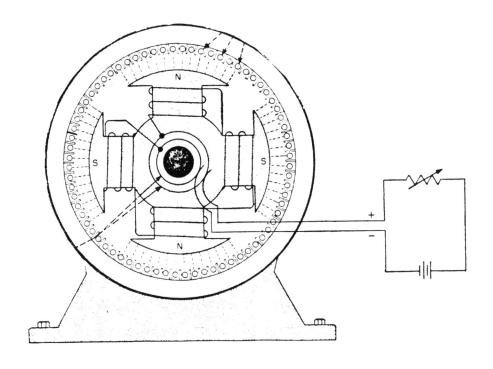

B. **Kinetic Energy** -- Electric Motor

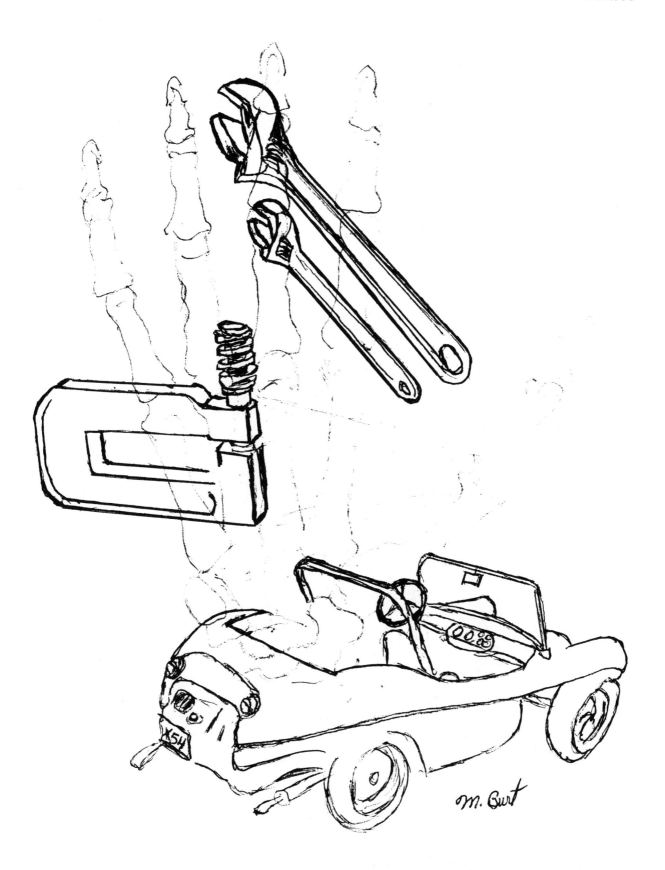

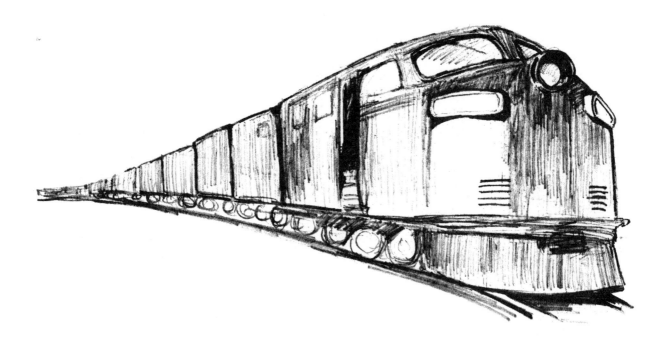

The Romance of the Rails

Prologue

The first American railroad was chartered in 1827; and almost immediately black Americans began designing and patenting basic devices for its operation and for the safety of both trainmen and passengers. Included were switches, couplings, semaphores, telegraph systems, boilers, and many other devices to further overload a beleaguered U.S. Patent Office. A number of these are described in this text.

Nowhere has there been such an inspired integration of a race into an industry, unless in the vineyards of southern Europe. And certainly nowhere else in modern history is there anything analogous to the importance of this transportation system in the overall development of a land and a culture. The relationship of the blackman to this vibrant matrix of ribboned steel, power, commerce, and history . . . may best be described as a "Romance of Unrequited Love."

There is a majestic beauty and a special insight into the character of the black . . . involved in these inventions — the wedding of human concern to inspired creation! There is also tragedy — as when, upon the advent of the diesel engine, the locomotive cab became too clean a place for a black fireman to work. There are the old, yellowed editions of the *Pittsburgh Courier* newspaper, acknowledging that as many were shot out of locomotive cabs by snipers, as were asked to leap by a concerned "Casey Jones."

In any case, the final elimination of blacks from status positions on the railroads of America was eventually accomplished by the rewriting of the union constitutions. But, during the first three-score years . . . blacks were able to leave an indelible mark.

Black Inventors of America

Subsequent pages delineate the engineering skill and background of man and some of his creations. Viewing the tragic foreclosure on black participation and today's news-media reports of services retrogression, along with the I.C.C. investigations of rising accident rates and equipment failures, one is prompted to question: "What great and viable system could the American Railways be today had this marvelous black talent been given the role it had so clearly earned?"

It is necessary to examine the pressures involved — pressures that were responsible for a peculiar but well-documented phenomena of 19th century America, where entire ethnic groups were violently displaced from their crafts and vocations. This was especially true in the case of the railroads, as well as in the craft unions. The greatest losses were suffered by blacks, Chinese, and Mexicans.

As successive waves of unskilled and destitute European immigrants arrived, few had the wherewithal or ability to compete with blacks in the trades or in business. Black carpenters, plumbers, ironworkers, masons, etc., had served 200 years of enforced apprenticeship — building mansions, roads, levees, docks, public buildings, bridges, canals, and countless other structures, often, it is true, at gunpoint.

As soon as the Reconstruction soldiers left for home, shrewd politicians and power-hungry manipulators saw their chance. They fanned the fires of frustration, racial antipathy, and status among the poor whites and ex-planters; they procured the faggot and the rope and the Klan; and in the end they delivered what they had promised: the status jobs of the blacks and White Supremacy!

The truth is (and this has been brought out in Supreme Court cases of the last two decades) that most "Jim Crow" laws in the South were not passed until the 1800's. Tennessee passed such a law in 1881, followed by Florida, Mississippi, Texas, Louisiana, and others.

The "Plessy vs. Ferguson" case, of 1896, and abolishment of this "separate but equal" doctrine in 1954, together reveal the time and the tenor of the transition.

Within the framework of this economic and social composite, we may now appraise a number of historic inventions in context and with a more complete perspective.

Andrew J. Beard

An older almanac reveals that there shone over the tiny town of Eastlake, Alabama, one momentous night in late November, a very full and portentous Southern moon. The next day the U.S. Patent Office was to grant a patent on the "Jenny-Coupler," a device that was to save the lives and limbs of thousands of the world's trainmen.

During years of labor in the local railroad yards, Andrew Beard had often come home heartsick over the latest tragic accident. Usually it happened this way: a man would run along the top of a freight train, climb down between two cars, hoping to drop a coupling pin in order to join the cars as they came together. The locomotive would back up, the cars would crash together and become firmly coupled — but too often at the expense of the unfortunate man's arm.

Over a long period of time, the young black laborer struggled to visualize an automatic linkage system that would obviate the involvement of a human limb in the final mating operation of the two cars. Often he was spurred by the personal impact of death or injury to a friend or neighbor. Then, late at might the tired but determined Beard would sit at his kitchen table and struggle over his concepts. How to attach the tail pin to the lock mechanism? How to position the operating rod to withdraw the lock and release the head? How to . . . How to . . . How to . . . ? And the finally, in the middle of the last decade of the 19th century, he produced a working model!

He filed his patent application in September, 1897; and it was granted two months later. He was paid $50,000 for his invention that same year by the New York firm. Refusing to let his lack of formal training in either engineering or metal working deter him, Andrew Beard had driven to his goal! Ingenuity and compassion had been wedded and would affect the entire world.

A. J. BEARD.
CAR COUPLING.

No. 594,059.   Patented Nov. 23, 1897.

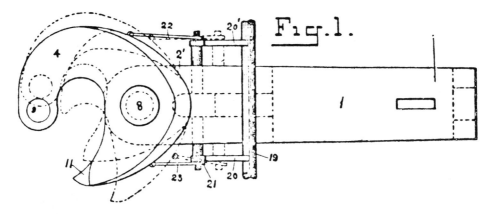

(No Model.)

A. J. BEARD.

CAR COUPLING.

No. 594,059. Patented Nov. 23, 1897.

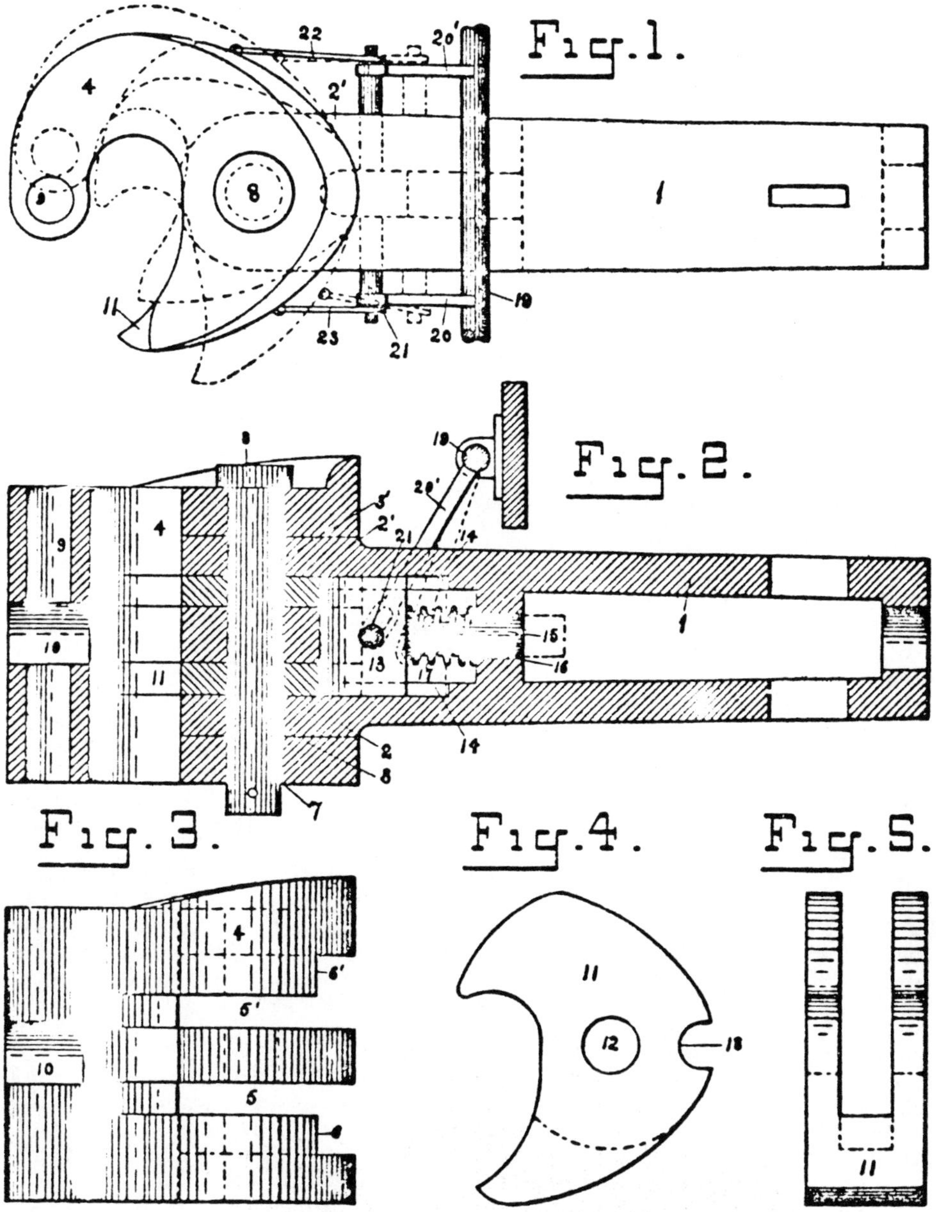
Fig. 1.
Fig. 2.
Fig. 3.
Fig. 4.
Fig. 5.

Witnesses
Jno. F. Fletcher
R. A. McAdory

Inventor
A. J. Beard
By his Attorney P. Byrne

UNITED STATES PATENT OFFICE

ANDREW JACKSON BEARD, OF EASTLAKE, ALABAMA.

CAR-COUPLING.

SPECIFICATION forming part of Letters Patent No. 594,059, dated November 23, 1897.

Application filed September 20, 1897. Serial No. 652,393. (No model.)

To all whom it may concern:

Be it known that I, ANDREW JACKSON BEARD, a citizen of the United States, residing at Eastlake, in the county of Jefferson
5 and State of Alabama, have invented certain new and useful Improvements in Car-Couplings; and I do hereby declare the following to be a full, clear, and exact description of the invention, such as will enable others skilled
10 in the art to which it appertains to make and use the same.

My invention relates to improvements in that class of car-couplings in which horizontal jaws engage each other to connect the cars;
15 and the objects of my improvement are, first, to provide a car-coupler of a simple and cheap form of construction, the coupler assembled in parts adapted to replace any of the pieces as desired; second, to provide a car-coupler
20 having the head and shank constructed in separate parts and pivotally connected by a pin, by which a new head or shank can readily be attached to replace a broken part; third, to provide an automatic car-coupling
25 having a head and side jaw pivotally attached to the shank, the head and jaw adapted to open and close in opposite directions to couple or uncouple the cars. I attain these objects by the mechanism illustrated in the accom-
30 panying drawings, in which—

Figure 1 is a top or plan view of my improved automatic car-coupler. Fig. 2 is a vertical sectional view of the same through the center. Fig. 3 is a detail vertical side view
35 of the head. Fig. 4 is a detail plan view of the side jaw. Fig. 5 is a front view of the same.

The draw-head shank 1 is made of any suitable metallic material, preferably of wrought or cast steel. The body of the shank is formed
40 to fit the usual car dimensions and is adapted to be attached to the car in the usual manner. Two lugs 2 2' are provided on the front end of the shank. The lugs extend forwardly from the shank and have pin-holes 3 3' pro-
45 vided therein.

The head 4 is made of cast-steel or other suitable metallic material. The head is provided with slots 5 5', formed therein to receive the jaw. Slots 6 6' are also provided
50 in the head to receive the lugs formed on the front end of the shank. A pin-hole 7 is formed through the head to receive the pin 8, the pin pivotally connecting the head and shank together. The usual pin-hole 9 is formed in the front of the head to connect with a link,
55 the usual slot 10 being provided to admit the use of a link, if desired.

The jaw 11 is made of cast-steel or other suitable metallic material, formed as shown, the tail-wings formed thereon being adapted
60 to fit the slots formed in the head. The jaw is provided with a pin-hole 12 to pivotally connect the jaw, in connection with the head, to the draw-head shank by the pin 8, as shown.

The head-lock 13 is made of suitable me-
65 tallic material, formed as shown. The lock slides in grooves 14 14', provided in the shank-lugs. A tail-pin 15 is formed on the lock. The tail-pin extends through a bearing 16, provided in the shank. A coiled spring 17 is
70 provided on the tail-pin. The spring pressing against the head of the lock keeps the same pressed forward to engage the concave recess 18, provided in the head and side jaw.

The operating-rod 19 extends across the end
75 of the car and is attached thereto by any of the usual methods. Any desired form of cranks can be formed on the ends of the rod. The rod ends or cranks are not shown in the drawings or any particular form claimed.
80

Two rigidly-connected levers 20 20' extend downwardly from the operating-rod 19. The levers are pivotally connected at their lower ends to the transverse bar 21, connected to the locking device. The rod 22 connects the
85 lock with the head. The rod 23 connects the lock-bar with the side jaw. The turning of the operating-rod to withdraw the lock and release the head also operates the connecting-rods to open the head and jaw, as shown by dotted
90 lines in Fig. 1. The head and jaw when open allow the draw-heads to come apart and uncouple the cars. The cars, if pushed together, recouple the draw-heads automatically.

Having thus described my invention, what
95 I claim as new, and desire to secure by Letters Patent, is—

1. In a draw-head, the combination with the shank having projecting lugs formed on the front end thereof, of the head having
100 slots formed therein to receive the shank-lugs, the jaw engaging in slots formed in the head, the pin pivotally connecting all the parts together, and the sliding locking device

2   594,059

to engage the recesses formed in the head and jaw, substantially as and for the purpose described.

2. In a car-coupling, the combination with the operating-rod having two downwardly-extending arms, the lower ends of the arms pivotally connected to a transverse bar attached to the locking device, of a rod connecting the head to the lock-bar, and a rod connecting the side jaw to the lock-bar, substantially as described.

In testimony whereof I affix my signature in presence of two witnesses.

ANDREW J. X BEARD.
his   mark

Witnesses:
    W. T. ROBINSON,
    P. K. McMILLER.

Granville T. Woods
(1856-1910)

From the subways of New York, to the "fruited plains" of the Midwest; from the Rockies to our Western shores; and, indeed, wherever else in the world that a "Song of the Rails" is meaningful . . . we are indebted to the prolific outpouring of electrical and mechanical genius from an Australian-born black man.

The parents of Granville T. Woods emigrated to the U.S. when he was sixteen. He had had little formal education, having been apprenticed out as a bellows-blower at the age of ten. But even so, his inquiring mind expanded this railroad yard job into an informal school.

In his early teens, he mastered the mechanics of the locomotive engine, even paying from his meager earnings for tutorage from the master mechanic. Consequently, when his family settled in Missouri, he was quickly employed as an engineer by the Iron Mountain Railroad. Later he became Chief Engineer aboard the British steamer, "Ironsides."

By 1880 he had established his own shop n Cincinnati, Ohio; and a few years later he became interested in thermal power and steam-driven engines.

He filed his first patent in 1890, on an improved steam-boiler furnace (the original is included in this text).

The inventions of this inspired black inventor were catholic: A telephone, which he sold to the Bell System; a telegraph system which enabled moving trains to communicate with each other and which was successfully used in 1885 on the New Rochelle Road.

In 1892, an electric railway system of his invention was operated at Coney Island, New York; and it was June 10, 1922, when he was granted a patent on the Automatic Air Brake — joining Andrew Beard as an inspired innovator in the field of railroad safety.

In all, Woods invented fifteen appliances basic to electric railways. His invention in 1900, however, served as entirely different field — an electric incubator for the hatching of chickens.

Edison, Bell, and the Westinghouse Company bought some of the devices he invented. Indeed, Woods brought two patent cases against the former; and in both cases, *he was able to prove that he had earlier rights to inventions claimed by Edison.* After the second loss to the black inventor, Thomas Edison offered him a position; but Woods turned it down, preferring to be his own master in the "Woods Electric Company."

Descriptions of the litigation and the confrontations between these two giants are colorful and fascinating.

Ward Harris, a well-known authority on Thomas Edison, left the world's most complete collection of inventions and writings by that inventor, when he died. The reader may wish to know that much pertinent information is available at 49 Fremont Street, San Francisco, California 94105.

Another black man was an original member of the famous "Edison Pioneers." This was electrical engineer Howard Latimer, whose work is listed briefly in the back of this book. In addition to his own inventions and patents, he did all of Alexander Graham Bell's drafting and redesigning of circuitry and otherwise assisted in his patent applications. Indeed, it was the formidable Latimer who was the Edison Company's "star" of patent defense cases; but the indomitable Woods nevertheless won the fruits of his genius and ceaseless labors.

Woods was given to almost poetic titling of his inventions and to descriptions of their benefits to humanity. Take for example, the "Synchronous Multiplex Railway Telegraph," of 1887; designed "for the purpose of averting accidents by keeping each train informed of the whereabouts of the one immediately ahead or following it, in communicating with stations from moving trains; and in promoting general social and commercial intercourse."

It is a remarkable achievement . . . that Granville T. Woods, who patented over a hundred and fifty electrical and mechanical inventions . . . was finally respected for "his remarkable knowledge of the intricate mathematics of electricity" . . . in a time of increasing racism and Jim Crow emphasis. The American Catholic Tribune, in 1888, described him as *the greatest electrician in the world.*

. . . sic transit gloria . . .

Granville Woods
Induction Telegraphy
November 15,1887
#373,915

Black inventor Granville Woods gave America (and American railroads) Induction Telgraphy — and all that it meant to the safety and efficiency of railroading since 1887.

Inventor Woods was responsible not only for the following patents, but for more than a hundred others as well:

Patent No. 299,894	June, 3 1884	Steam Boiler Furnace
Patent No. 667,110	January 29, 1901	Electric railway
Patent No. 678,086	July 9, 1901	Electric railway system
Patent No. 681,768	September 3, 1901	Regulating & controlling electrical translating devices
Patent No. 687,098	November 19, 1901	Electric railway
Patent No. 701,981	June 10, 1902	Automatic air brake
Patent No. 718,183	January 13, 1903	Electric railway system
Patent No. 729,481	May 26, 1903	Electric Railway
Patent No. 308,816(7)	December 2, 1884	Telephone transmitter
Patent No. 315,368	April 7, 1885	Apparatus for transmission of messages by electricity
Patent No. 364,619	June 7, 1887	Relay instrument
Patent No. 366,192	July 5, 1887	Polarized relay
Patent No. 366,192	August 16, 1887	Electro-mechanical brake
Patent No. 371,241	October 11, 1887	Telephone system and apparatus
Patent No. 371,655	October 18, 1887	Electro magnetic brake apparatus
Patent No. 373,383	November 15, 1887	Railway telegraphy
Patent No. 373,915	November 29, 1887	Induction telegraph system
Patent No. 383,844	May 29, 1888	Overhead conducting system for electric railway
Patent No. 385,034	June 26, 1888	Electro motive railway system
Patent No. 386,282	July 17, 1888	Tunnel construction for electric railway
Patent No. 387,839	August 14, 1888	Galvanic battery

No. 701,981.

G. T. WOODS.
AUTOMATIC AIR BRAKE.
(Application filed Feb. 5, 1901.)

(No Model.)

Patented June 10, 1902.

3 Sheets—Sheet 1.

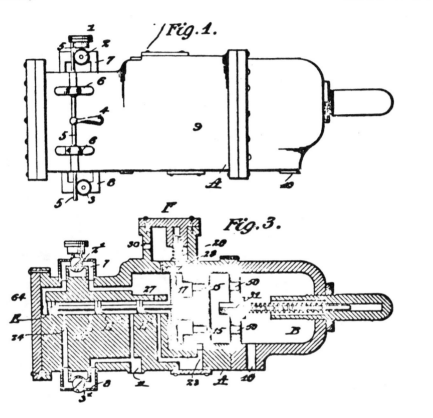

Fig.1.

Fig.3.

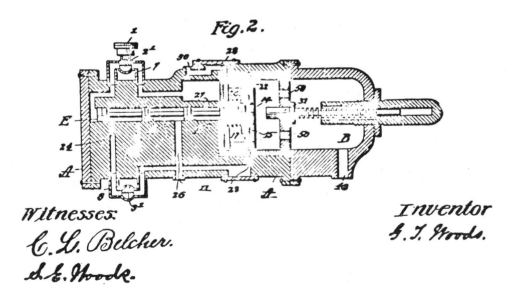

Fig.2.

Witnesses:
C. G. Belcher.
S. E. Woods.

Inventor
G. T. Woods.

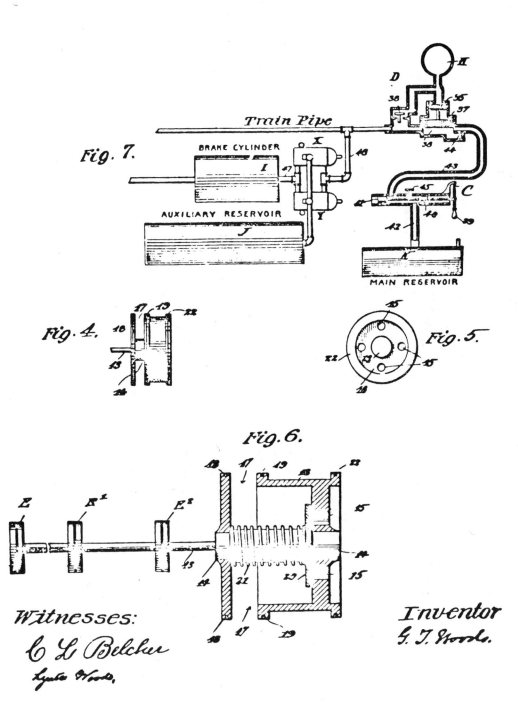

No. 701,981.

G. T. WOODS.
AUTOMATIC AIR BRAKE.
(Application filed Feb. 5, 1901.)

(No Model.)

Patented June 10, 1902.

3 Sheets—Sheet 2.

Train Pipe

Fig. 7.

BRAKE CYLINDER

AUXILIARY RESERVOIR

MAIN RESERVOIR

Fig. 4.

Fig. 5.

Fig. 6.

Witnesses:
C. L. Belcher

Inventor
G. T. Woods.

No. 701,981.

G. T. WOODS.
AUTOMATIC AIR BRAKE.
(Application filed Feb. 5, 1901.)

(No Model.)

Patented June 10, 1902.

3 Sheets—Sheet 2.

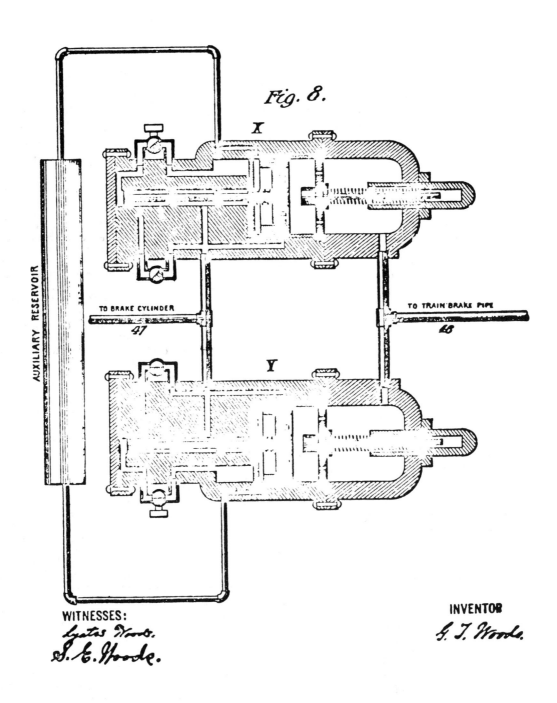

Fig. 8.

X

Y

AUXILIARY RESERVOIR

TO BRAKE CYLINDER

47

TO TRAIN BRAKE PIPE

48

WITNESSES:

INVENTOR

UNITED STATES PATENT OFFICE.

GRANVILLE T. WOODS, OF NEW YORK, N. Y., ASSIGNOR, BY MESNE ASSIGN-
MENTS, TO THE WESTINGHOUSE AIR BRAKE COMPANY, OF PITTSBURG,
PENNSYLVANIA, A CORPORATION OF PENNSYLVANIA.

AUTOMATIC AIR-BRAKE.

SPECIFICATION forming part of Letters Patent No. 701,981, dated June 10, 1902.

Application filed February 5, 1901. Serial No. 46,080. (No model.)

To all whom it may concern:

Be it known that I, GRANVILLE T. WOODS, a citizen of the United States, and a resident of New York, in the county of New York and
5 State of New York, have invented certain new and useful Improvements in Automatic Air-Brakes, of which the following is a specification.

My present invention relates to the pecul-
10 iar construction and arrangement of the valves and other parts of an automatic brake mechanism which is preferably operated by compressed air.

My invention has for one of its objects to
15 compel a positive action of each brake when the same is expected to "go on," to stop the car, or to "come off," and thereby release the car.

Railway accidents are reported frequently
20 as being due to the failure of the air-brake systems; and it is one of the objects of my present invention to avoid some of the weak points of the familiar systems in daily use.

The brake system in general to which my
25 present improvements are shown applied is that in common use and includes, in addition to the brake-cylinder, auxiliary reservoir, and train-pipe, the usual equipment on the loco-motive—such as an air pump or compressor,
30 a storage-tank, and an engineer's valve—all of which parts are familiar to persons skilled in the construction and operation of brake mechanisms. In addition to the parts named a complete automatic air-brake system in-
35 cludes as one of its essential elements a valve mechanism located on each car and serving to control the admission and escape of air in the brake-cylinder for effecting the application and release of the brakes. Such valve mech-
40 anism is popularly known as "triple-valve" mechanism, and the present improvements relate more particularly to the valve element or part of the brake system and introduces a peculiar mode of operation, notwithstanding
45 the fact that I employ the usual pressure of air when causing a gradual application of the brakes and also when a "quick-action" or emergency stop is being made, the grad-ual application being produced by energy
50 from the auxiliary reservoir; but the quick

action is caused by an initial air-supply from the train-pipe to the brake-cylinder and a final air-supply from said auxiliary reservoir to the said brake-cylinder.

It is well known to those skilled in the pro-
55 fession of locomotive-running that if an air-brake on one car fails to go on it not only causes the loss of the braking effect of that particular car-brake, but it also causes the other brakes of the train to lag or go on slowly,
60 because the air-pressure in the train-pipe in such cases is not reduced quickly, there be-ing one less brake-cylinder to take a portion of said air from said train-pipe, and thereby accelerate the remaining valve apparatus. It
65 is also well known that if an emergency stop is made at a time when the brake system is normal the time and distance required in which to make the stop is short, while the same train will require a longer time and dis-
70 tance in which to cease its motion when the brake system is slightly abnormal. The dif-ference between the short time and distance demanded in the one case and the longer time and distance required in the other case
75 is often the span between life and death. To insure a far more positive, powerful, and a much quicker action than is possible to be ob-tained by the use of the familiar systems afore-said, I have provided a novel construction and
80 arrangement of the main or double-acting-valve part, the valve of which may be of any suitable kind and combined with the valve-piston part (I term the combination a "valve device") and the various ports, so that not
85 only will the valves and other parts coöperate, but they may be incorporated with the valve mechanism of the well-known Westinghouse air-brake system or any form of air-brake which will operate interchangeably with said
90 Westinghouse system. Furthermore, by the addition of one of my valve devices to each car which is at present supplied with the said Westinghouse system or the New York air-brake apparatus or some similar equip-
95 ment a system will thereby be produced which will embody the majority of the most valuable features of my present invention, and thus add greatly to the reliability of the common air-brake equipment.
100

To more fully understand my invention, reference is made to the accompanying drawings, in which—

Figure 1 is a side view of the outside case of my invention. Fig. 2 illustrates a sectional view of the casing and some of the parts of Fig. 1. In Fig. 3 is shown a sectional view of some of the parts and a full side view of other parts of a modification of my invention. Fig. 4 is a side view of the valve-piston part. Fig. 5 is a face view looking from right to left of said valve-piston part. Fig. 6 is an enlarged sectional view of the valve device illustrated in Figs. 2 and 8. Fig. 7 illustrates one way of connecting up the brake-system, so that if one of the valve devices or a valve should fail to operate the other valve device will operate, so that the brake-cylinder will be certain to receive the air-pressure required for its operation. Fig. 8 is a sectional view of the valve devices and their casings when such are arranged as shown in Fig. 7.

In Fig. 1 the part indicated by numeral 1 is an air vent or box which is filled with cotton or some other suitable porous material, so that when the air is drawn through the same from the outside atmosphere, as hereinafter set forth, the porous material then acts as a filter, serving to prevent grit or dirt from entering the valve-chamber or valve-space which is within the valve-case. Valves 2 and 3 are controlled by moving handle 4 upward or downward. The direction in which said handle is moved will of course depend upon which of the air-passages are to be opened and which are to be closed. Said handle connects with valves 2 and 3 through rod or bar 5, as shown in the drawings. 6 6 are guides for bar 5. The ends of said bar and the outer ends of said valves are provided with teeth, so as to produce what is termed a "rack-and-pinion" movement. 7 and 8 are the passage-ways or air-pipes controlled by valves 2 and 3.

In Figs. 2, 4, 5, 6, and 8 I have shown the valve device which controls the various ports. When I use the words "valve device" I mean the valve-piston and the main valve acting as different parts of one device, one of said parts controlling the admission of air from the auxiliary reservoir to the brake-cylinder, while the other part governs the air-admission from the train-pipe to the brake-cylinder. The valve device or, in other words, the valve-like device and the parts connected thereto are more clearly illustrated in Fig. 6, which is the preferred form, enlarged so that the parts may be more readily indicated and understood, and the same may be used as a reference to assist in the explanation of Fig. 2, &c. The preferred construction of said apparatus is as follows: The main-valve part, as shown in this case, is what is technically termed a "piston-valve" and the piston part to which said valve is connected and by which it is moved is (in the present art)

technically termed a "valve-piston," each part being so named because of its peculiar construction, movements, and the work it performs. The main-valve part herein shown has three partitions E E' E². These are fixed upon stem 13, which in turn is firmly attached to the hub 14 of the valve-piston part. The valve-piston part of the valve device may be made in one piece, as shown in Fig. 3, or it may be composed of several parts, as shown in Fig. 2. The valve-piston part has one or more ports or passages 15, leading through the web or wall 16 into piston-port 17 in the body of the said piston, thence out at the port-opening between the wall 18 and flange 19. In Figs. 2, 6, and 8 the said ports 15 are closed one way by check-valve 20, which is held to its seat by spring 21. In practice the space between flanges 19 and 22 is sufficiently great to normally cover port 23, which (when open or uncovered by the valve-piston part) leads from the train brake-pipe through passage 11 to the brake-cylinder. The three partitions E E' E² of the main-valve part are arranged in the following manner: Partitions E and E' are so arranged that the restricted port 24 is normally between them, while the restricted exhaust-port 25 is always between them. Port 26 is always between partitions E' and E², while port 27 is normally between partition E² and wall 18. Now as the valve device moves from the extreme end of its path at the left to the other extreme end of its path to the right (as in emergency stops) then partition E moves to another position between ports 24 and 25. Partition E' remains in its normal pathway between ports 25 and 26, while partition E² takes up a new position between port 27 and wall 18, at which time the brakes will go on. When the engineer causes the valve device to move to "take off" the brakes, said partitions take up their normal positions to the left. In Fig. 3 the check-valve 20 is arranged in a valve-box outside of the case A. In this arrangement valve 20 normally covers port 28. When valves 2' and 3' are open, as in Fig. 2, then passage 7 leads from the auxiliary-reservoir opening 30, around through valve 2' to opening 11, thence to the brake-cylinder.

In some brake systems the auxiliary reservoir is charged to the same restricted port or passage which communicates between the auxiliary reservoir J and the brake-cylinder I. In my apparatus as illustrated in Figs. 2, 3, &c., the passage 28 is for charging the auxiliary reservoir J, and said passage is arranged as a "by-pass"—that is, it provides a large direct passage around the restricted port (through which air is supplied from the auxiliary reservoir to the brake-cylinder) directly to the opening 30, leading to the auxiliary reservoir, thus avoiding the slow reservoir-recharging process used in said familiar systems. By the arrangement herein set forth the engineer is permitted to recharge the auxiliary reservoir while the brakes are on or applied. This new and valuable feature is the result of the peculiar arrangement of the ports and valves, and its value is great when a long heavy train is running downgrade and the engineer desires to keep the train under control. It is well known that when the brakes are "on" the air constantly leaks from the brake-cylinder. Hence the necessity of recharging the auxiliary reservoir while the brakes are on.

It will be observed that valves 2' and 3' (shown in Fig. 3 and also in the upper portion X of Fig. 8) are set to obstruct the passages 7 and 8, which said valves control, while in Fig. 2 and also the lower part Y of Fig. 8 valves 2' and 3' are set to permit an open way through said passages. These valves are never set to obstruct the air-passages except when two valve devices and their inclosing cases communicate with one brake-cylinder, as shown in Figs. 7 and 8, one of said valve devices acting as a graduating main valve, while the other valve device acts as an emergency-valve only, operating only when emergency stops are being made. Whenever two valve devices are coupled up, as shown in Figs. 7 and 8, one of the said devices is converted into a differential piston—that is to say, the valves 2' and 3', while being turned, as shown in said figures, so as to obstruct the passages 7 and 8, leading to or from the valve-piston part, will simultaneously open a passage leading from the outer end E of the main-valve part, through box or vent 1, to the outer atmosphere. Now if air under pressure is admitted to both sides of the valve-piston part the total number of pounds useful pressure upon the said piston-surface next to partition E^2 will be less than the total number of pounds useful pressure on the piston-surface next to the adjusting-stem 31, this difference in the useful pressures being due to the counteracting influence of the surface of partition E^2, which is so exposed as to oppose the pressure against the piston-surface next thereto. It will be noted that as partition E is not exposed to the air-pressure when said air-passages are obstructed the end surface thereof cannot be taken into the calculation. The surfaces of partition E^2 and piston-wall 18 should be so proportioned that the arrangement as a differential piston will remain quiescent unless required to act when making an emergency stop, at which time about twenty pounds reduction is made in the train-pipe air-pressure, so that the preponderance of pressure will be on the auxiliary-reservoir side of said piston part. Then the auxiliary-reservoir air-pressure will move the said differential piston back toward the right until it reaches the extreme limit of its path, as hereinafter explained, thus acting absolutely independent of any motion (or the effect of any motion) which the associate graduating main-valve device may make.

In Fig. 7 I have shown a main air-pressure reservoir, an auxiliary reservoir, a brake-cylinder, two valve devices X and Y, an engineer's valve C, and an automatic discharge-limit valve, which is connected in the train-pipe at point D between the engineer's valve and the brake apparatus. The object of said discharge-limit valve is to prevent the escape of more than a predetermined amount of air through the action of the engineer's valve when an emergency stop is to be made. It is well understood that when an emergency stop is to be made the engineer suddenly discharges twenty pounds (more or less) from the train-pipe. When said reduction of train-pipe pressure takes place, the valve mechanism should act promptly to admit air from the train-pipe and also from the auxiliary reservoir to the brake-cylinder. Now when an emergency stop is required the engineer has no time to gage the escaping air. Therefore a much greater reduction of the air-pressure takes place than such cases demand, thus reducing the amount of compressed air which should have passed from the train-pipe into the brake-cylinder instead of being discharged into the atmosphere, and thereby reducing the efficiency of the brake system and adding to the time required to effect a stop. The arrangement of the discharge-limit valve is as follows: Parts 35 and 36 form the two heads of a differential piston, said heads being connected by a stem, as shown, or head 35 may be made in the form of a plunger, if so desired. This said piston moves within a case or cylinder in the usual way, as shown. The usual vent is indicated at 37. An air-reservoir is shown at H and a check-valve at 38. The operation is as follows: The lever 39 of the engineer's valve is shown in position to admit air under pressure from reservoir K through pipe 42 into the space between the valve-heads 40 and 41, thence through pipe 43, under piston-head 36, then to the train-pipe. Meanwhile some of the air forces its way past check-valve 38 and accumulates in reservoir H and the tubular communications immediately connected therewith. Thus there will be a pressure against both ends or heads of said differential piston, and when the pressure in said reservoir H is equal to that in the train-pipe the check-valve 38 will be seated and the air in reservoir H will be "entrapped" or confined. The under surface of head 36 being greater in square inches than the upper surface of head 35 permits the preponderance of pressure to move the piston upward to the position shown in the drawings. Now if the engineer pulls lever 39 to the right until it reaches the limit of its travel by being brought up against screw 45 then air will rush out from the train-pipe and past the outer end of head 41. As soon as the pressure in the train-pipe has been reduced to the predetermined limit the preponderance of pressure will then be against the small head 35 of said differential piston, and therefore said piston will be

Black Inventors of America

4

forced down to its seat. In other words, the pressure of the said entrapped air is not reduced by the reduction of the train-pipe pressure. Therefore when the train-pipe pressure is reduced to a point where its total number of pounds pressure against head 36 is below the total number of pounds pressure exerted against head 35 by the entrapped air then the said piston will be forced down to its seat, and thereby limiting the reduction of the train-pipe pressure by closing or obstructing the train-pipe at the appropriate moment, thus permitting the air to be transferred while at its highest permissible pressure from the train-pipe to the brake-cylinder. When the train-pipe is to be recharged, lever 39 is moved to the position shown in the drawings. Then air will pass from the reservoir K, as hereinbefore set forth, until it reaches passage 44, through which the air has access to the under side of piston-head 36, which will then be forced upward until it reaches the position shown in the drawings. Air will in the meantime recharge the train-pipe and the auxiliary reservoirs. It will be noted that the discharge of air is automatically limited or stopped independently of the engineer's valve. When connecting up a single valve device to a car, connections are made between the train-pipe and valve-case A, as follows: A branch pipe leads from said train-pipe and connects wit' said case at point 10. Another connecting-pipe is placed between the brake-cylinder and said case at point 11, while a third pipe connection is supplied between the auxiliary reservoir and said case at point 30. The train-pipe has the usual connections from car to car, &c. When a single valve device is used, the operation is as follows: To charge the auxiliary reservoir and prepare the brakes for action, air at about seventy pounds pressure is permitted to flow from the main reservoir K through the train-pipe and its connections into opening 10, (of valve-case A,) thence through chamber B, passages 50, ports 15, around check-valve 20, through piston-port 17, port 28, passage 30, to the auxiliary reservoir. A portion of the air passes along through passage 7, valve 2, to the outer side of partition E. In the meantime the valve device has been forced to the extreme left of case A. Thus the brake-cylinder is cut off from the train-pipe and the auxiliary reservoir, and the exhaust-passage is open between the brake-cylinder and the atmosphere. When it is desired to apply the brake gradually, the handle 39 of the engineer's valve will be moved for a moment to such a position that communication between the main reservoir K on the engine and the train-pipe will be closed and an escape-passage is open between the train-pipe and the atmosphere. Thereby the air-pressure in the train-pipe will be reduced about five pounds. This reduction of pressure on the train-pipe side of the valve-piston part disturbs the balance previously existing on the opposite sides thereof, resulting in establishing a preponderance of air-pressure on the auxiliary-reservoir side, and the air delivered from the auxiliary reservoir through passage 30 and acting upon the valve-piston part causes the valve device to move toward the right. This movement will continue until partition E has passed to the right of port 24, thus allowing auxiliary-reservoir air to flow through passages 30 and 7, valve 2', to port 24, thence through passage 8 and valve 3', passage 11, to brake-cylinder, where it acts upon the piston thereof to cause the brakes to go on. When by reason of the flow of air into the brake-cylinder the pressure in the valve-chamber and auxiliary reservoir has been reduced to or below that of the train-pipe, a slight return or leftward movement of the valve device will be produced, (by the combined action of the train-pipe pressure and the adjusting-stem 31), sufficient to cause the partition E to rest upon and close port 24, and thus close communication between the valve-chamber and the brake-cylinder and confine the air admitted within the latter. In case it is desired to gradually increase the air-pressure in the brake-cylinder the above operation is repeated. To permit the air in the brake-cylinder to escape and "let off" or release the brakes, the air-pressure in the train-pipe is restored or increased by a proper and well-known movement of the engineer's valve. The increase of pressure in the train-pipe causes the valve device to move leftward to the limit of its path, when it will occupy the position shown in Fig. 2, &c., thereby placing restricted port 24 in communication with exhaust-port 25 and allowing the brake-cylinder air to escape. It should be understood that in practice I cause the passage which directly connects with exhaust-port 25 to be much more restricted than any of the other said passages, thereby causing the exhaust from the brake-cylinder to be very gradual. At the same time the restoration of the pressure in the train-pipe will unseat check-valve 20, (after the piston-port 17 registers with port 28,) and air from the train-pipe will flow into the auxiliary reservoir, recharging it for future use. The pressure in the auxiliary reservoir will then equal that in the train-pipe, when the check-valve 20 will be seated by its spring 21. When it becomes necessary to recharge the auxiliary reservoir while the brakes are on, the engineer moves his valve suddenly and connects the main reservoir K to the train-pipe. This causes the valve devices to move quickly to the full limit of their paths toward the left, thus placing the auxiliary reservoir in communication (through large passages) with the fully-charged train-pipe, thus causing the auxiliary reservoir to be charged in an instant. The passage from the brake-cylinder through the exhaust (said passage being open while said recharging was being accomplished) is quite small or restricted at the ports. Therefore the air which

40

is confined in said brake-cylinder will have escaped but slightly before said auxiliary reservoir was fully charged and the engineer discharged some air from the train-pipe as when first applying the brakes. Thus it will be noted that the brake-cylinder was permitted to receive a second supply of air-pressure before the first supply was exhausted. When it becomes necessary or desirable to apply the brakes quickly and with full power for an emergency stop, the engineer's valve will be moved to close the communication between the main reservoir K and the train-pipe and open the latter to the atmosphere and produce a sudden reduction of pressure of about twenty pounds in the train-pipe. The effect of this sudden diminution of pressure in the train-pipe is immediately manifest at the discharge-limit valve (which acts instantly) and the nearest valve device or that on the first car, causing the valve device to be moved by the higher pressure of auxiliary-reservoir air quickly toward the right to the end of its path. Then port 23 registers with the piston-port 17 of the valve-piston part, and thereby placing the auxiliary reservoir and the train-pipe in communication with the brake-cylinder and closing the exhaust-port. The following passages are now open: A pathway leads from opening 30 through passage 7, valve 2', port 24, passage 8, valve 3' to opening 11, thence to the brake-cylinder. Another communication is from opening 30 through ports 27 and 26 to opening 11, thence to the brake-cylinder. Yet another air-pathway is from opening 10 through chamber B, opening 50, ports 15, piston-port 17, and port 23 to opening 11, thence to the brake-cylinder. The auxiliary reservoir and the train-pipe being thus brought suddenly into communication with the brake-cylinder passages will cause check-valve 20 to be immediately unseated and train-pipe air will pass along said path between opening 10 and opening 11, thence directly into the brake-cylinder, thus effecting the quick initial application of the brakes and also a further reduction of pressure in the train-pipe that will be sufficient to accelerate the action of the valve mechanisms on the cars following. The valve-piston part will in the meantime be held to its outward position (toward the right) by the relatively higher air-pressure from the auxiliary reservoir, which is delivered through large passage 30, while the transmission of the auxiliary-reservoir air from passage 30 to the brake-cylinder is retarded by having to pass through the restricted port 24. After the air-pressures in the train-pipe and the brake-cylinder have equalized auxiliary-reservoir air will continue to flow from the auxiliary reservoir into the brake-cylinder until there is an equalization of air-pressure in both said auxiliary reservoir and brake-cylinder. Then adjusting-stem 31, together with the train-pipe pressure, will move the valve device toward the left until

partition E covers port 24. It will be seen that the valve-piston part is moved in one direction by the auxiliary-reservoir pressure, the return movement being produced by the train-pipe pressure or adjusting stem 31, or both combined, as hereinbefore set forth. It will be noted that by restricting the flow of auxiliary-reservoir air a considerable volume of train-pipe air is allowed to flow freely into the brake-cylinder, notwithstanding the admission to the brake-cylinder at the same time of a small volume of the auxiliary-reservoir air under a higher pressure. An appreciable period of time is required to raise the pressure in the brake-cylinder to that in the auxiliary reservoir, and it is during this interval and before the pressure in the brake-cylinder is raised to that in the train-pipe that the air in the latter is free to enter the brake-cylinder. To release the brakes, a sufficient amount of air is admitted from the train-reservoir K to the train-pipe to overcome the resistance of the auxiliary-reservoir pressure and friction of the valve mechanism and move the valve device to the end of its stroke, (toward the left, as shown in Fig. 2, &c.,) and thereby establish a communication between the brake-cylinder and the atmosphere by way of the exhaust-passage 25. It will be noted that ports 26 and 27 are brought into use only when an emergency action of the valve device takes place. In making a gradual stop the valve device is not moved far enough to the right to allow ports 26 and 27 to communicate with each other.

In Fig. 8 I have illustrated an arrangement in which two valve devices (such as shown in Fig. 2) are so coupled up that both parts X and Y are permanently and independently connected to the train-pipe, the brake-cylinder, and the auxiliary reservoir; but the valve devices of each part X and Y control the various ports at the appropriate time, and the action of one of said valve devices will always be absolutely independent of the condition or action of the other valve device. In other words, the valves 2 and 3 (part X) being set to obstruct the air-passages 7 8, which said valves control, and valves 2' 3' (part Y) permitting the passage-ways, which they control to be open, then the valve device of part X must act as a differential valve device, as previously set forth herein, while the valve device of part Y will act in the manner hereinbefore set forth, describing the operation of a single valve device. In making either a gradual stop or an emergency stop the engineer's valve is manipulated in exactly the same manner as when controlling the Westinghouse system, that being the same manner in which my present single valve device is controlled. In making the gradual stop the valve device in part Y controls the air-pressure necessary to make the stop and acts as previously set forth herein. In the meantime the valve device in part X will remain quiescent for the reasons already set forth herein.

When an emergency stop is to be made, air is discharged from the train-pipe, thereby reducing the pressure about twenty pounds. The preponderance of air-pressure will then be
5 on the auxiliary-reservoir side of both of said valve devices. Therefore they will immediately move toward the right to the ends of their paths. This will open five paths through which the air pressure will travel to reach the
10 brake-cylinder. The said paths are as follows: The train-pipe discharges into the brake-cylinder through ports 15 in both valve devices, and thence through ports 23 to the brake-cylinder. Another path leads from
15 openings 30 (in both valve cases) through ports 27 and 26 (part X) to the brake-cylinder, and a fifth path leads from opening 30 (part Y) through passage 7, valve 2', around to port 24, thence through valve 3' to the brake-cyl-
20 inder. To release the brakes, air is admitted as previously described, and the valve devices will move to their normal position to the left, at which time the air confined in the brake-cylinder escapes through one outlet only—
25 viz., through passage 8', valve 3', restricted port 24, and exhaust-port 25. The partition E in part X is exposed to the atmosphere through vent 1. It will be observed from the foregoing description that if one of the valve
30 devices failed to perform its work the other device would act promptly. This is because the train-pipe pressure and the auxiliary-reservoir pressure act upon the pistons of said valve devices simultaneously, independently,
35 and differentially. From the explanation herein set forth it will be noted that I may use one of said parts (X or Y) for gradual stops, while the other part may be used for quick action or emergency stops only. Either
40 part X or Y (when arranged as illustrated in Figs. 7 and 8) may be transformed at will by means of handle 4 from a graduation valve device to an emergency valve device, and vice versa.
45 I do not limit my invention to any particular kind or shape of valve.

I am aware that it has been proposed to control the direct or emergency communication between the train-pipe and the brake-cylin-
50 der by means of a supplemental valve and piston which is unconnected with the main-valve piston, but upon the movement of which said supplemental piston (to obtain motion) must depend for a supply of air-pressure, and
55 such construction, which involves an operation and arrangement different from that of my invention, I therefore hereby disclaim.

What I claim is—

1. In an air-brake system, the combination
60 of a train-pipe having a direct communication with two adjacent piston or valve chambers, a communication between an auxiliary reservoir and a brake-cylinder, a communication between the train-pipe and the brake-cylin-
65 der, a restricted exhaust-passage between the brake-cylinder and the atmosphere, a valve device in one of said chambers and adapted

to control said exhaust and also admit air from the auxiliary reservoir to said brake-cylinder when such valve device is in its normal con-
70 dition, and a normally inert valve device in the remaining or second of said chambers and adapted to admit air-pressure sufficient to apply the brakes independently of the condition of the first-mentioned valve device in an
75 emergency application, the said restricted exhaust being adapted to restrict the escape of air from the brake-cylinder if the first-mentioned valve device should fail to close the exhaust when an emergency-brake applica-
80 tion is made.

2. In an air-brake system, the combination of a passage from the train-pipe, a passage from the brake-cylinder which is smaller or more restricted than said train-pipe passage,
85 and a valve device, consisting of a valve connected with a ported piston, coacting with both of said passages and controlling communication between said train-pipe passage and the auxiliary reservoir and also between said
90 brake-cylinder and the exhaust whereby when it is desired to release the brakes, the train-pipe air will have a passage through said ported piston and thence through a large passage-way to the auxiliary reservoir, the brake-
95 cylinder air will have a passage-way through a valve-controlled restricted passage to the atmosphere.

3. A valve apparatus for automatic air-brakes, having in combination two ports or
100 passages communicating with the brake-cylinder, one of said passages being small and from the auxiliary reservoir and the other a large passage from the train-pipe, so that the flow of auxiliary-reservoir air is restricted as
105 compared with the flow of train-pipe air when both are flowing to the brake-cylinder during an emergency brake action, a ported piston actuated in both directions by air-pressure, a stem having one end suitably con-
110 nected with said piston, and a suitable valve operated by said stem to open and close the passage from the auxiliary reservoir while said piston controls the valved passage from the train-pipe to the brake-cylinder and opens
115 the same for emergency stops only.

4. In an air-brake system, the combination of a passage from the train-pipe, a passage from the auxiliary reservoir which is smaller or more restricted than said train-pipe pas-
120 sage, and a valve device consisting of a valve which is mechanically connected to and moved in both directions by a ported piston, the said valve device coacting with both of said passages and controlling communication
125 between them and the brake-cylinder whereby, when an emergency application of the brakes is desired the train-pipe air and the auxiliary-reservoir air, the former at a lower pressure than the latter, will both have pas-
130 sages open to the brake-cylinder as follows: said train-pipe air-passage being through said piston and thence through a by-path in the valve-case, the said auxiliary-reservoir

air-passage being through another path in the valve-case and controlled by said valve.

5. A valve mechanism for automatic air-brakes having in combination, a passage leading to the brake-cylinder from the train-pipe, a passage leading to the brake-cylinder from the auxiliary reservoir, which is smaller or more restricted than said train-pipe passage, a ported piston actuated in one direction, by pressure from the train-pipe to close said train-pipe passage, and actuated in the opposite direction by pressure from the auxiliary reservoir to open said train-pipe passage, a stem having one end suitably connected with said piston, and a valve suitably connected with said stem and moved thereby to control said passage between the auxiliary reservoir and the brake-cylinder, while said piston controls the passage between said train-pipe and the brake-cylinder and opens said passage for emergency stops only.

6. In an automatic air-brake system, the combination, with the train-pipe, an auxiliary reservoir, and a valve device, of a second valve device which is adapted to act absolutely independent of the action or inaction of the first-mentioned valve device and only when emergency brake applications are made, both of said valve devices being adapted to admit air from the auxiliary reservoir to brake-cylinder, and a passage from said train-pipe to said brake-cylinder, and controlled by said second valve device.

7. In an air-brake system, the combination of a train-pipe, two valve devices communicating therewith, the piston parts of both of said devices being constantly under the train-pipe air-pressure and each of said devices being adapted to operate absolutely independent of either the action or inaction of the other and each of such devices being adapted to control a passage leading from the auxiliary reservoir to the brake-cylinder.

8. In an air-brake mechanism, the combination of a train-pipe having a connection to a valve-device chamber or casing, a communication between said chamber or casing and an auxiliary reservoir, a communication between said chamber or casing and a brake-cylinder, and a normally inert differential piston-valve device located within said chamber or casing and adapted to act when making emergency stops only, and establish a check-valved communication between said train-pipe and said brake-cylinder, the piston of said valve device being actuated by auxiliary-reservoir air-pressure in one direction to open or establish the latter communication, and moved by train-pipe air-pressure to cut off or close said communication, during such movements said device operating free from any other valve device.

9. In an air-brake system, the combination of a train-pipe, an auxiliary reservoir, a brake-cylinder, two valve devices adapted to act absolutely independent of each other, air communication between said train-pipe and the auxiliary reservoir, air communication between said train-pipe and said brake-cylinder, air communication between said auxiliary reservoir and said brake-cylinder and a restricted air-passage between said brake-cylinder and the atmosphere, each of said valve devices being adapted to influence the air movement from said auxiliary reservoir to said brake-cylinder, one of said valve devices operating only during emergency applications of the brakes.

10. In an air-brake system, the combination of a valve device, substantially as described, having a ported piston mechanically connected with a valve, a chamber or case for said piston, a chamber for said valve, a passage from the train-pipe to said piston-chamber, a passage from said piston-chamber to the auxiliary reservoir, a passage from said piston-chamber to the brake-cylinder, a restricted passage from said auxiliary reservoir to the brake-cylinder, and a restricted passage from said brake-cylinder to the exhaust-opening, the said piston when at one end of its cylinder forms a part of a communication between said train-pipe and said auxiliary reservoir, said valve in the meantime forming a part of a communication between said brake-cylinder and said exhaust-opening, but when said piston is at the other end of its cylinder it becomes a part of a communication between said train-pipe and said brake-cylinder, said communication being open for emergency stops only, and said valve, in the meantime, opening a communication between the auxiliary reservoir and said brake-cylinder.

11. In an air-brake mechanism, the combination of a train-pipe having a tubular connection to two adjacent valve-device chambers or casings, a tubular connection from each of said chambers or casings to a brake-cylinder, a tubular connection from each of said chambers or casings to an auxiliary reservoir, a passage from the brake-cylinder to the atmosphere, a graduating-valve device located within one of said chambers or casings, and a normally inert differential piston-valve device located within the other chamber or casing, the latter valve device being adapted to operate when making emergency stops only, and control the communication between said train-pipe and said brake-cylinder, each piston of said valve devices being actuated by auxiliary-reservoir air-pressure in one direction to open or establish said communications and moved by train-pipe air-pressure in the opposite direction to close or cut off said communications, in operation said valve devices acting absolutely independent of each other.

Signed at New York, in the county of New York and State of New York, this 17th day of January, A. D. 1898.

GRANVILLE T. WOODS.

Witnesses:
E. RILEY,
ORY CANE.

Your school bus is safer than before . . .

. . . because Richard B. Spikes' last great invention was in the form of a "fail-safe" brake for motor vehicles!

This device (Patent No 3,015,522, January 2, 1962), was invented shortly before his death. Remarkably enough, this invention, combining the best in both hydraulic and electrical approaches, was executed by an elderly Spikes who, because he was going blind, also had to invent a drafting machine for the blind in order to finish his work.

The author knew Richard Spikes personally and is deeply indebted to his brother, Benjamin Spikes, owner of the Mecca Mortgage Company, in Los Angeles, for locating the following materials:

Richard B. Spikes

This great creative talent was responsible for the following inventions:

The modern version of the Railroad Semaphore, in 1906.[1] The automatic car washer *and* auto directional signals, in 1913 (Pierce Arrow). The beer keg tap, in 1910 (Milwaukee Brewing Company). The continuous contact trolley pole for electric railways in 1919 (San Francisco "Key Line").

Patent No. 1590,557	Combination milk bottle opener and bottle cover.	June 29, 1926
Patent No. 1828,753	Method and apparatus for obtaining average samples and temperature of tank liquids.	October 27, 1931
Patent No. 1,889,814	Automatic gear shift.	December 6, 1932
Patent No. 1,936,996	Transmission & shifting thereof.	November 28, 1933
Patent No. not found	Self-locking rack for billiard cues.	approximately 1910
Patent No. not found	Automatic shoe shine chair which folds up for storage.	approximately 1939
Patent No. not found	Multiple barrel machine gun.	approximately 1940

---

1   Some patents are not included here, because of litigation; or they were so basic in nature that redesigning and refiling procedures are in process.

Nov. 28, 1933.   R. B. SPIKES   1,936,996

TRANSMISSION AND SHIFTING MEANS THEREFOR

Filed Dec. 17, 1932   2 Sheets-Sheet 1

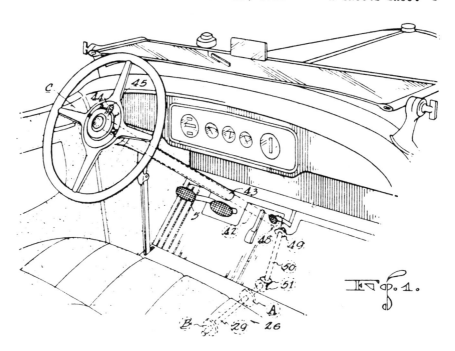

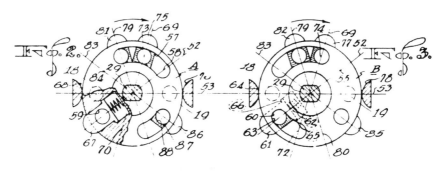

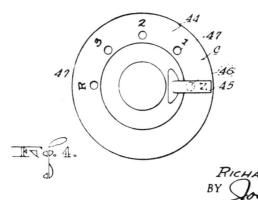

INVENTOR.
RICHARD B. SPIKES.
BY Joseph I. Cole
ATTORNEY

Nov. 28, 1933.   R. B. SPIKES   1,936,996

TRANSMISSION AND SHIFTING MEANS THEREFOR

Filed Dec. 17, 1932   2 Sheets—Sheet 2

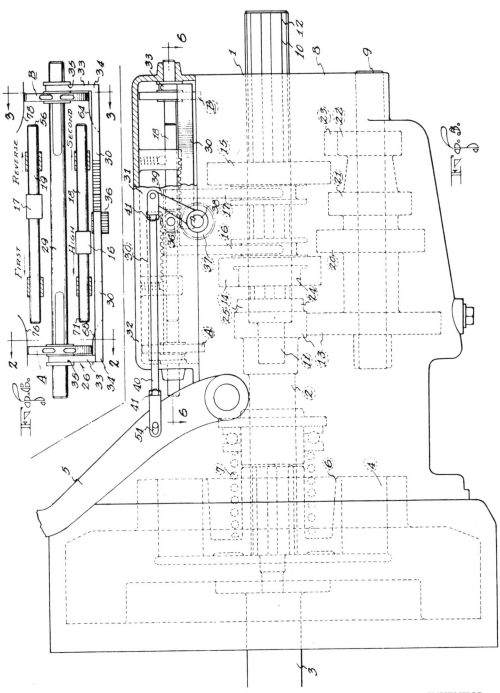

INVENTOR.
RICHARD B. SPIKES.
BY Joseph J. Cole.
ATTORNEY

Patented Nov. 28, 1933

1,936,996

UNITED STATES PATENT OFFICE

1,936,996

TRANSMISSION AND SHIFTING MEANS THEREFOR

Richard B. Spikes, San Francisco, Calif.

Application December 17, 1932
Serial No. 647,772

8 Claims. (Cl. 74—58)

The present invention relates to improvements in transmissions and shifting means therefor, and has among its objects the provision of a transmission having a gear shifting selector associated therewith adapted to be operated from the driver's compartment of a vehicle through a selective indicator, and arranged for automatically shifting the gears of the transmission selected upon disengaging the conventional clutch.

The driver moves the indicator at any convenient time for a contemplated change in gear speed, and upon depressing the clutch pedal the clutch is first disengaged during the initial movement of the clutch pedal, and further movement acts to move the gears from a previous shift into neutral position and thereafter the gears set up in the new selection are actually moved into driving engagement. The operation takes place in a single movement of the clutch pedal and the steps follow without interruption.

It is particularly proposed to accomplish the shifting of the gears through mechanical means, which are simple in construction, durable and efficient for carrying out the operation of the transmission.

Moreover, I propose to provide a selector that may be readily attached to a conventional transmission with but slight alteration in the latter. The selector is adapted for mounting on the transmission housing and beneath the floor of the vehicle, and this leaves the driver's compartment free and unobstructed.

Other objects will appear as the specification proceeds, and the novel features will be particularly set forth in the appended claims.

For a better understanding of my invention, reference should be had to the accompanying drawings, forming part of this application, in which:

Figure 1 is a fragmentary perspective view of an automobile having my transmission embodied therein;

Figures 2 and 3 are sectional views taken along lines 2—2 and 3—3, respectively, of Figure 6;

Figure 4 illustrates the indicator which I employ;

Figure 5 is a side elevation of the transmission with parts broken away so as to disclose the interior thereof; and

Figure 6 is a section along line 6—6 of Figure 5.

Although I have shown only the preferred form of my invention, it should be particularly understood that various changes or modifications may be made within the scope of the appended claims without departing from the spirit of the invention.

In carrying my invention into practice I provide a transmission indicated generally at 1, and having a stub shaft 2 rotatably mounted therein that is adapted to be connected to a source of motive power 3 by means of a conventional clutch 4, the latter being operated by a foot pedal 5. The clutch that I have illustrated is of the multiple disc type, in which the plates are caused to separate upon depressing the pedal for disengaging the driven element 6 of the clutch from the driving source. The clutch further includes a spring 7 arranged for returning the plates to driving position upon releasing the pedal. It will of course be appreciated that any suitable type of clutch may be employed in association with the transmission.

Within the transmission housing 8 is also mounted a countershaft 9 in parallel relation with a driven shaft 10, the latter being axially aligned with the stub shaft and having one end thereof journalled in the stub shaft as at 11, while the opposite end extends from the housing at 12 for connection to the propeller shaft in the usual manner. The countershaft is rotated by the stub shaft through gearing 13, the gears of which are in constant mesh.

The driven shaft of the transmission has a pair of selective gears 14 and 15 splined thereon, which are adapted for axial sliding along the shaft by means of forks 16 and 17, respectively, the fork 16 being anchored to a shifting rod 18 and the fork 17 fixed to a second shifting rod 19.

It will be noted from Figure 5 that the countershaft above referred to has driving gears 20, 21 and 22 secured thereto which provide for the different speed ratios and direction of turning between the shafts 2 and 10. Upon sliding the gear 15 into mesh with gear 21 by moving the shifting rod 19 to the left in Figure 6, the transmission is thereupon shifted into "low", while a movement of the rod in the opposite direction will effect "reverse", an idler pinion 23 being used for interposition between the gears 15 and 22.

In shifting the transmission into "second" or "intermediate" the gear 14 is placed in driving engagement with the gear 20, and this is accomplished by imparting endwise movement of the shifting rod 18 to the right in Figure 6, the fork 16 in this case being actuated. "High" or "third" is effected by connecting the shafts 2 and 10 directly through the medium of the usual jaw clutch arrangement 24, rod 18 being moved to the left for shifting the gear 14 into telescoping relation with the teeth 25 projecting from the pinion on the shaft 2.

While I have described this particular type of a transmission, it will be appreciated that other transmissions may be employed, and the free-wheeling and synchro-mesh features which are now well known in the art may be incorporated in the transmission described hereinbefore.

For moving the shifting rods 18 and 19 as previously mentioned I provide a gear shifting selector 26 that is particularly illustrated in Figure 6, and comprising in its structural features a revolvably mounted shaft 29 having a pair of discs A and B splined thereon and arranged to be moved toward or away from each other. The means for moving these discs consist of racks 30 which are slidably secured to the side 31 of a housing 32, forks 33 being extended from the rack ends 34 into engagement with annular grooves 35 which are fashioned in the hubs of the discs.

In Figures 5 and 6 I show a pinion 36 interposed between the racks that is adapted to be turned in a clockwise direction for drawing the discs toward each other. The pinion is turned by means of a gear 37 that is secured to a stub shaft 38, the latter having a lever 39 fixed thereto. This lever is disposed on the exterior of the housing 32 and is connected to the foot pedal 5 of the clutch through a link 40. The length of the link may be adjusted at 41 so as to swing the lever 39 through the proper arc as hereinafter mentioned. The operation of the selector in shifting the rods 18 and 19 will be set forth later in the specification.

Turning now to Figure 1, it will be seen that I provide a tubular member 42 that extends downwardly through the standard 43 of the steering mechanism, this member having a hand-grasping finger thereon that is made for riding over a scale 44 of the indicator designated generally at C. The finger is indicated by the numeral 45, and is provided with a spring-press pin or ball 46 arranged for entering recesses in the scale for holding the finger in adjusted position, although the finger may be advanced over the scale with but slight pressure being applied to the finger. The recesses are shown at 47.

It will be noted that the finger is disposed in "neutral" position in Figure 4, and as the finger is advanced over the scale, the same is successively advanced through "low", "second", "third" and "reverse" positions.

The lower end of the tubular member 42 is provided with a pinion 48 which is in mesh with a second pinion 49 on the shaft 50, the latter in turn being connected to the shaft 29 of the selector 26 by means of level gearing 51. Upon moving the indicator finger to "low" position, the discs A and B in the selector are turned together by the rod or shaft 29 through the mechanism just described so as to bring the lines 52 in Figures 2 and 3 into coincidence with the center line 53, the latter representing a horizontal plane through the centers of the shifting rods 18 and 19 and the shaft 29.

With the selector thus set up for shifting into "low", the driver presses on the pedal 5, and during the initial movement thereof, the clutch is first disengaged before the lever 39 begins to swing, this being accomplished by means of a lost motion connection 54 between the link 40 and the pedal. As the discs A and B are further drawn towards each other, the solid wall portion 55 of the disc B butts against the end 56 of the shifting rod 19, and as the pedal 5 is moved still further, the rod 19 projects through the slot 57 in the disc A in the area indicated at 58, and

the gears 15 and 21 are thereupon moved into driving engagement. During this movement, the shifting rod 18 remains in normal position, the disc A being slotted at 59 and the disc B at 60 so as to telescope over the rod 18.

However, should the transmission already be in "second", the opening 60 in the disc B will be closed by means of a gate 61 that is mounted for radial movement in the disc. The gate normally is urged outwardly by a spring 62 until the opening 63 therein is brought into registration with the slot or opening 60. As the disc B is turned for setting up "low", the outer rounded end of the gate 61 strikes a cam 64 so as to move the gate inwardly and temporarily close the opening 60. The gate is retained in this position and acts to shift the rod 18 back into "neutral", whereupon the gate clears the end of the cam 64 (see Figure 6), and the spring 62 then moves the gate outwardly until the opening 63 therein is positioned for telescoping over the rod 18. At this time, the discs have been moved through one-half of their stroke, and during the remainder of the stroke the rod 19 is moved into "low", while the rod 18 remains stationary. The outward movement of the gate is limited by means of stops 65 striking against shoulders 66.

Assuming now that the transmission is driving in "high" and it is desired to shift into "low". In this case the gate 67 on the disc A acts in a similar manner in cooperation with a cam 68 to disengage the transmission from "high" gear and return the rod 18 to normal before the rod 19 begins to move into "first" or "low". Likewise, if the transmission is running in "reverse" the disc B will return the rod 19 to a position for disengaging the gear 15 from the pinion 23, and during further movement of the selector discs, the rod 19 is advanced so as to shift the gear 15 into mesh with the gear 21 for constituting "low".

It will thus be apparent that regardless of which speed the transmission may be running in due to a previous shift, that the slidable gear on the shaft 10 will first be entirely disengaged before the new combination for "low" speed is effected, and this entire operation is accomplished during a single depression of the pedal 5. As the specification continues, it will be shown that the same is true of all of the other speeds of the transmission.

Particularly it will be seen in Figure 6 that the discs A and B, when in extended position, are arranged beyond the furthest movement of the shifting rods 18 and 19. Therefore, if one of the rods is moved for engaging a gear speed, and thereafter the pedal 5 is released, the discs will be disposed so as to clear the end of the shifted rod and thus allow the operator of the vehicle to set up a new speed, which may be effected any time subsequently and at his convenience and desire.

When the driver wishes to shift into "second", he first turns the indicator finger 45 over the scale to "second", and this swings the discs A and B in a clockwise direction in Figures 2 and 3 until the line 69 coincides with the line 53. This presents the solid wall portion 70 of the disc A into position for abutting the end 71 of the rod 18 upon moving the discs toward each other. At the same time the disc B is turned for allowing the rod 18 to be projected through the slot 60 in the area indicated at 72 (see Figure 2). The rod 19 during this operation remains stationary, if in normal position, since the opening 73 in the disc A and the opening 74 in the disc B are arranged for allowing the discs to telescope thereover. The spring-pressed gate 75 on the disc A, in cooperation with the cam 76 serves to return the rod 19 to normal, if the transmission should already be in "low"; while the gate 77 on the disc B cooperates with its cam 78 for disengaging the transmission from "reverse" in a similar manner should the transmission be so engaged from a previous shift. Likewise, if the transmission is running in "high", the disc A acts to return the rod 18 to normal before engaging the gears for "second".

In setting up the selector for a contemplated change to "third", the driver turns the finger 45 to the proper position on the scale 44, and this rotates the selector discs until the line 79 is turned clockwise into registration with the line 53. This brings the wall area 80 of the disc B into position for shifting the rod 18 to the left in Figure 6 for effecting "high" speed. In this case, the gate 81 on the disc A and the cam 76 serve to return the gears constituting "low" into disengagement as the selector discs are drawn toward each other, if these gears have been previously meshed. If the transmission is driving in "reverse" the gate 82 and the cam 78 first disengages the gears forming this speed before the new combination is completed.

On the other hand, if the transmission is running in "second" and the selector has been moved for shifting into "high", the disc B during the first half of its movement toward the disc A disengages the gears 14 and 20 completely before the clutch elements 24 and 25 are meshed for "high".

When the driver contemplates a change to "reverse", the finger 45 is moved accordingly, and this rotates the selector discs a still further step than for "high", and brings the lines 83 into the horizontal plane indicated by the numeral 53, and thereafter the selector discs are drawn toward each other. The walled portion 84 on the disc A abuts the rod 19 and moves the latter into a position for shifting the transmission into "reverse". During this operation, the gate 85 coacts with its cam 64 and serves to disengage the transmission in the event that the gears forming this speed are in mesh. In a similar manner, the gate 86 on the disc A strikes its cam 63 during the setting of the selector for a change into "reverse" and closes the opening 87 in the disc until such time as the rod 18 is returned to normal, whereupon the cam is cleared and the opening 88 is brought into registration with the opening 87, and thus the rod 18 is permitted to remain stationary during further movement of the discs.

The returning of gears to "neutral" which may be engaged is accomplished by bringing the indicator finger 45 to the proper marking on the indicator, and this places the selector discs in the relative position illustrated in Figures 2 and 3. Upon depressing the pedal 5, the rods 18 and 19 are shifted into normal position; that is, into the position shown in Figure 6. As the pedal is released, the discs separate so as to position the same from the ends of the shifting rods by a distance equal to the movement required for engaging the gears.

Having thus described the various parts and operation of my transmission, the functioning thereof may be readily understood. The driver sets the indicator at any convenient time for a contemplated change in speed, and upon depressing the pedal 5, the clutch is first released, and further movement operates to disengage the old combination of gears should the transmission be in driving position. Still further movement engages the newly selected gears. These steps follow without interruption and during a single operation of the clutch pedal.

Having thus described the various parts and operation thereof, what I desire to secure by United States Letters Patent is:

1. In a gear shifting mechanism, parallel shifting rods movable endwise from normal, a shaft mounted therebetween, companion selectors slidable on the shaft and rotatable therewith, the selectors being arranged on the opposite ends of the rods, and including portions selectively engageable with the rods, means for turning the shaft to set the selectors, means on the selectors for carrying a previously shifted rod back to normal and being thereupon releasable, means for effecting the release, and means for moving the selectors toward each other to effect the shifting.

2. In a gear shifting mechanism, shifting rods movable endwise from normal, companion selectors arranged in confronting relation and on opposite ends of the rods, means supporting the selectors for angular and axial movements, the selectors having portions selectively abuttable the rods to move the latter, means for turning the selectors to set the same, means on the selectors movable into position to return a previously shifted rod to normal, and having means coacting therewith to release the returning rod when the latter has been carried to normal, and means for moving the selectors axially.

3. In a gear shifting mechanism, shifting rods movable endwise from normal, companion selector discs arranged on opposite ends of the rods, means mounting the discs for angular and axial movements, the discs having slotted portions for telescoping over the rods and made to abut one of the rods at a time with an unslotted portion, means for turning the discs to set the latter, means on the discs to carry a previously shifted rod back to normal, means for thereupon releasing the returned rod, and means for moving the discs axially to effect the shifting.

4. In a gear shifting mechanism, a pair of selector discs arranged in confronting relation and having slots therein, means mounting the discs for angular and axial movements, shifting rods supported between the rods for telescoping through the slots, means for closing certain of the slots upon turning the discs so as to engage the rods as selected, means for adjusting the discs angularly, and means for moving the discs axially toward and away from each other.

5. In a gear shifting mechanism, a selector disc having slots therein, gates movably carried on the disc for closing certain of the slots and projecting from the disc periphery, means mounting the disc for angular and axial movements, means for moving the gates into open position relative to their respective slots, and cams extending axially of the disc for closing the gates as the disc is turned and for holding the gates closed until the disc has been moved axially to clear the end of the cams.

6. In a gear selecting and shifting mechanism, a selector disc having rod-receiving openings, means mounting the disc for angular and axial movements, means for closing certain of the openings as the disc is turned so as to present abutments when the disc is subsequently moved

4 **1,936,996**

axially, and means for turning the disc to set the latter.

7. In a gear selecting and shifting mechanism, a selector disc having rod-receiving openings, means mounting the disc for angular and axial movements, means for closing certain of the openings as the disc is turned so as to present abutments when the disc is subsequently moved axially, means for moving the disc angularly to effect the closing, and means for reopening the openings after a predetermined axial movement of the disc.

8. In a gear shifting mechanism, shifting rods movable endwise from normal, companion selectors mounted on opposite ends of the rods and in confronting relation, means supporting the selectors for angular and axial movements, the selectors having portions selectively abuttable the ends of the rods to move the latter, means for turning the selectors for setting the same, means movable into active position upon turning the selectors made to carry a previously shifted rod back to normal upon drawing the selectors toward each other, further inward movement of the selectors abutting the latter against the rod selected to effect shifting thereof, and means for operating the selectors toward and away from each other.

RICHARD B. SPIKES.

Black Inventors of America

More of the blacks who dreamed and engineered the American Railroad System!

Bell, L	Locomotive smoke stack	May 23, 1871	115,153
Blackburn, A. B.	Railway Signal	January 10, 1888	375,362
Brown & Latimer	Water closets for railway cars	February 10, 1874	147,363
Burr, W. F.	Switching device for railways	October 31, 1899	636,197
Butler, R. A.	Train alarm	June 15, 1897	584,540
Byrd, T. J.	Improvement in car-couplings	December 1, 1874	157,370
Cherry, M. A.	Street car fender	January 1, 1895	531,908
Clare, O. B.	Trestle	October 9, 1888	390,753
Jackson, W. H.	Railway switch	March 9, 1897	578,641
Jackson, W. H.	Railway switch	March 16, 1897	593,665
Purvis, W. B.	Electric railway	May 1, 1894	519,291
Purvis, W. B.	Magnetic car balancing device	May 21, 1895	539,542
Purvis, W. B.	Electric railway switch	August 17, 1897	588,176
(Purvis also patented 10 paper bag machines between 1884 and 1894.)			
Richey, C. V.	Car coupling	June 15, 1897	584,650
Richey, C. V.	Railroad switch	August 3, 1897	587,657
Richey, C. V.	Railroad switch	October 26, 1897	592,448
Robinson, E. R.	Electric railway trolley	September 19, 1893	505,370
Robinson, E. R.	Casting composite	November 23, 1897	594,286
Robinson, J. H.	Life saving guards for locomotives	March 14, 1899	621,143
Robinson, J. H.	Life saving guards for street cars	April 25, 1899	623,929
Romain, A.	Passenger register	April 23, 1889	402,035
Shanks, S. C.	Sleeping car berth register	July 21, 1897	587,165

Nor did these geniuses neglect the horse and buggy!

Brown, L. F.	Bridle bit	October 25, 1892	484,994
Brown, O. E.	Horseshoe	August 23, 1892	481,271
Byrd, T. J.	Improvement in holders for reins for horses	February 6, 1872	123,328
Byrd, T. J.	Apparatus detaching horses from carriages	March 19, 1872	124,790
Byrd, T. J.	Improvement in neck yokes for wagons	April 30, 1872	126,181
Coates, R.	Overbook for horses	April 19, 1892	473,295
Davis, W. D.	Riding saddles	October 6, 1896	568,939
Mendenhall, A.	Holder for driving reins	November 28, 1899	637,811
Outlaw, J. W.	Horseshoes	November 15, 1898	614,273
Ricks, J.	Horseshoe	March 30, 1886	338,781
Ricks, J.	Overshoes for horses	June 6, 1899	626,245

Creators of Industry and Jobs

Some folks say, "You have to earn your way in America"

Prologue

The American industrial complex is a swinging, ringing, rhythmic scene. "And how could it be otherwise?" you may ask, with the following pages as a kind of Ebony Witness. To fully assess the creative, black impact in terms of today's "Dow-Jones Index," as it were (that is, to "nitty-grittitize the structure," as Howard University students would say)...one would need to have on hand at least three of the "Bibles" of commerce:

1. The "Dictionary of Occupational Titles," published by the U.S. Department of Labor. This is a coded compilation and description of all the existing jobs and crafts in American industry.

2. The "Standard Industrial Classification Index,"[2] published by the U.S. Department of Commerce. This listing performs a similar function; but covers types

---

2   The first two books may be obtained from the Superintendent of Documents, Washington, DC 20402.

of Industries, Farming, Financial Institutions, and all other commercial activities of Americans.

3. The "Encyclopedia of Associations," published by the Gale Research Company of Detroit. Volume 1 is a roster of all the nationally organized groups in the United States, including all of the Industrial, Trade, Financial, and Union Organizations on the American scene.

Then, if you had an IBM 360 . . . and a Honeywell 1250 . . . and a Control Data unit . . . along with several other digital computers — then you might be able to figure out how much money the black men in this chapter have made for many, many Americans.

"Sugar is sweet and so are you" . . . but Norbert Rillieux made it that way — for millions of people who have taken home wages, dividends, fees, and profits, to the tune of billions of dollars, since 1846. It was then that the young, black engineer patented the Sugar Refining Process that revolutionized the Industry (Patent No 4879, December 10, 1847).

"Baby, your feets too big" . . . but Jan Matzeliger did something for everybody's feet, all over the world, when he came up with the fantastic Automatic Lasting Machine. New England has never been the same since — and neither has the proportion of personal income spend for shoes.

This invention had the secondary effect of opening the eyes of engineering and businessmen around the world . . . to what an organized application of this black's technique for mass production could do for both industry and consumers of the world. This is the one where the "mountain came to Mahomet." But those in the Patent Office just could not believe it when they opened the mail! And, after journeying to Lynn, Massachusetts, to view the "Thing," it still took them six years to understand it and to grant the patent (Patent No. 459,899, September 22, 1891).

"I'm beginning to see the light" . . . Lewis H. Latimer did just that, giving us the carbon filaments which made light bulbs possible on a mass production basis! (And incidentally helped Edison get off the ground.) Shortly afterwards, Edison invited Latimer to become a member of the group (Patent No. 252,386, June 17, 1882).

"Well you push the middle valve down" . . . but the Industrial Revolution would never have really made it if Elijah McCoy's father hadn't gotten by all those police dogs and "split" from "slavesville."

McCoy was born free, in Canada; and in 1872 began patenting the line of lubricating valves that made all this swinging, rhythmic industrial scene possible. His valves were so good and so essential to the smooth operation of the world's machinery (which kept getting bigger and bigger, and faster and faster) that this black man's name became part of colloquial English: "The Real McCoy."

These men are just a small segment of the black engineering renaissance. Knowledge of their accomplishments may have some relationship to Equal Job Opportunity, even to marches by their grandchildren, who would like to participate.

The very pertinent statistics, appearing below, were taken from the *1963 Census of Manufacturers*.

	Gross Sales
Code 3111, Leather Tanning & Finishing	$ 758,000,000
Code 3131, Boot & Shoe, Cut stock & Findings	229,300,000
Code 3141, All Footwear, except House Slippers	2,249,000,000
TOTAL[3]	$3,236,300,000

	Number	**Wages**
Totals for all employees, shoe & leather industries, 1899	54,551	25 mil.
Totals for all employees, shoe & leather industries, 1963	31,417	163 mil.
Auxiliary Gross Product: Wholesale, retail, advertising, etc., 1963	25,000	135 mil.

---

3   Does not reflect the proliferation of *auxiliary dollar functions* for distribution, advertising, banking, finance, and factoring, transportation, etc.; or for the corollary inputs to urban development and other socio-economic factors.

Jan Matzeliger

Jan Matzeliger was born in Paramaribo, Dutch Guiana, of parents who were former slaves. A slender and erect young man, known for a keen sense of humor, he began work in a Lynn, Massachusetts, shoe factory in 1877. Here he was shocked to find that one shoe alone took hours to complete. The reason for this was that hand lasters had to painstakingly pleat the leather and fitted uppers to the soles. To young Matzeliger it seemed incredible that by 1877 no machine had been devised for the operation. He decided immediately that he was the man who could solve the problem.

There seems to have been a common pattern to the makeup of these black inventors: initiative, resourcefulness, independence, and a tremendous drive and will to surmount obstacles . . . the unconquered spirit!

Matzeliger promptly rented a room over the Old West Lynn Mission. Here he constructed prototypes of his ideas, using scraps of wood, old cigar boxes, and improvised tools. After several years of experiment and much trial and error, he felt that he was on the right track. By using an old forge, abandoned by a local blacksmith, he was able to mold the needed gears and cams.

By 1883, he had evolved a fantastic piece of machinery, which combined so many different operations that it could *manufacture an entire shoe in one minute*. His invention was an immediate success. Its adoption created *thousands of new jobs*, where before only a few master craftsmen were required. *Shoe prices were cut* and *wages doubled*. Thousands of white immigrants left their European poverty to come to work in the prosperous industry created by this black innovator. Exports quickly jumped from one million pair to eleven million pair per year. Within five years, *Lynn, Massachusetts, became the world's largest shoe manufacturing center.*

For reasons undetermined, the Patent office delayed its stamp for six years and Jan Matzeliger sold his Patent to Sydney A. Winslow, who promptly founded the United Shoe Company.

In just a few years, Winslow bought up 40 smaller companies, hired hundreds of workers and increased the value of his product from a mere $220,000 to $242,631,000!

The Automatic Shoe Last Machine was patented on September 22, 1891, Patent No. 459,899. Other patents include:

Patent No. 415,726	November 26, 1899	Mechanism for Distributing Tacks
Patent No. 421,954	February 25, 1892	Nailing Machine
Patent No. 423,937	March 25, 1892	Tack Separating Mechanism

(No Model.)   10 Sheets—Sheet 1.

J. E. MATZELIGER, Dec'd.
G. W. MOULTON, EXECUTOR.
LASTING MACHINE.

No. 459,899.   Patented Sept. 22, 1891.

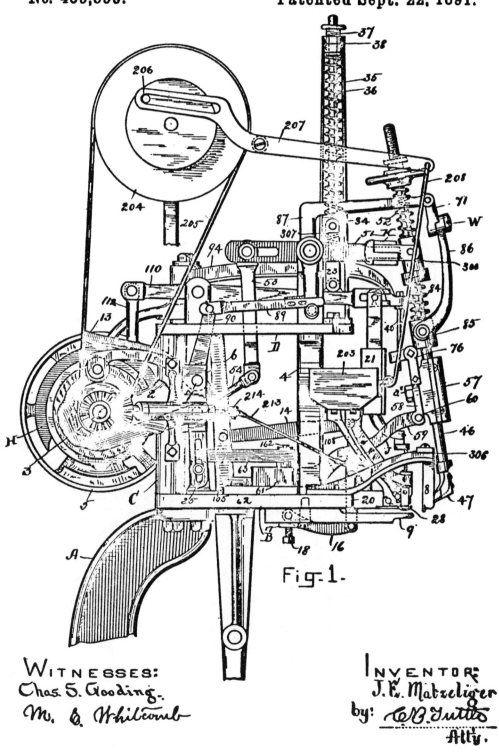

Fig. 1.

WITNESSES:
Chas. S. Gooding.
M. B. Whitcomb

INVENTOR:
J. E. Matzeliger
by: C. B. Tuttle
Att'y.

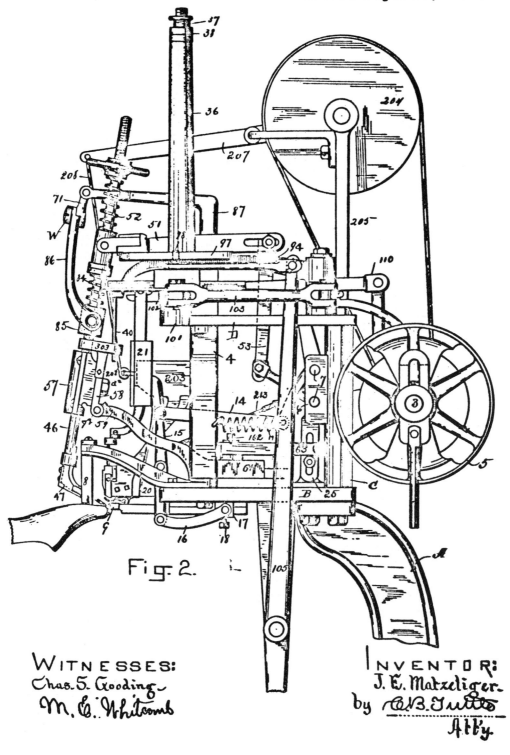

(No Model.)

J. E. MATZELIGER, Dec'd.
G. W. MOULTON, EXECUTOR.
LASTING MACHINE.

No. 459,899.

10 Sheets—Sheet 2.

Patented Sept. 22, 1891.

Fig. 2.

WITNESSES:
Chas. 5. Gooding
M. E. Whitcomb

INVENTOR:
J. E. Matzeliger.
by C. B. Tutts
Att'y.

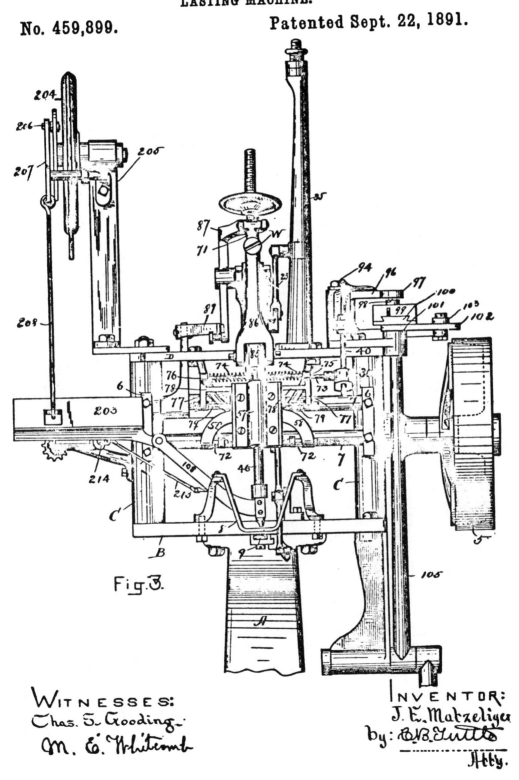

J. E. MATZELIGER, Dec'd.

G. W. MOULTON, EXECUTOR.

LASTING MACHINE.

No. 459,899.   Patented Sept. 22, 1891.

Fig.3.

WITNESSES:
Chas. S. Gooding.
M. E. Whitcomb

INVENTOR:
J. E. Matzeliger
by: B.B. Tutts
Atty.

(No Model.)   10 Sheets—Sheet 4.

J. E. MATZELIGER, Dec'd.
G. W. MOULTON, EXECUTOR.
LASTING MACHINE.

No. 459,899.   Patented Sept. 22, 1891.

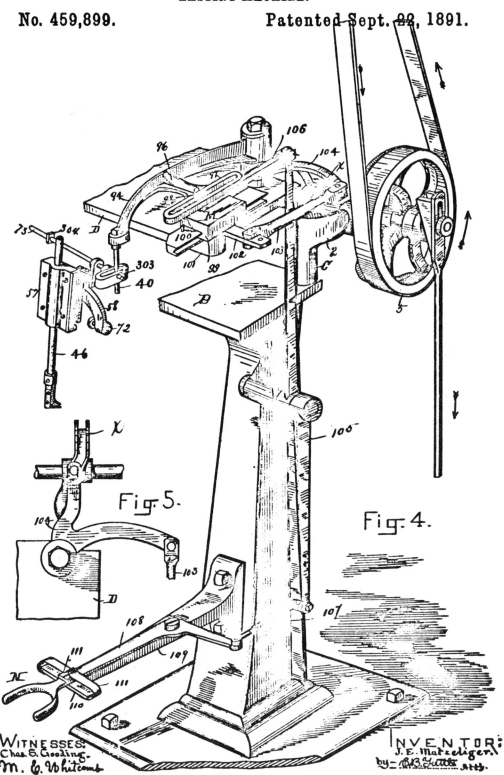

Fig. 5.

Fig. 4.

WITNESSES:
Chas. S. Gooding.
M. C. Whitcomb

INVENTOR:
J. E. Matzeliger.
by B. B. Little Atty.

(No Model.)   10 Sheets—Sheet 5.

J. E. MATZELIGER, Dec'd.
G. W. MOULTON, EXECUTOR,
LASTING MACHINE.

No. 459,899.   Patented Sept. 22, 1891.

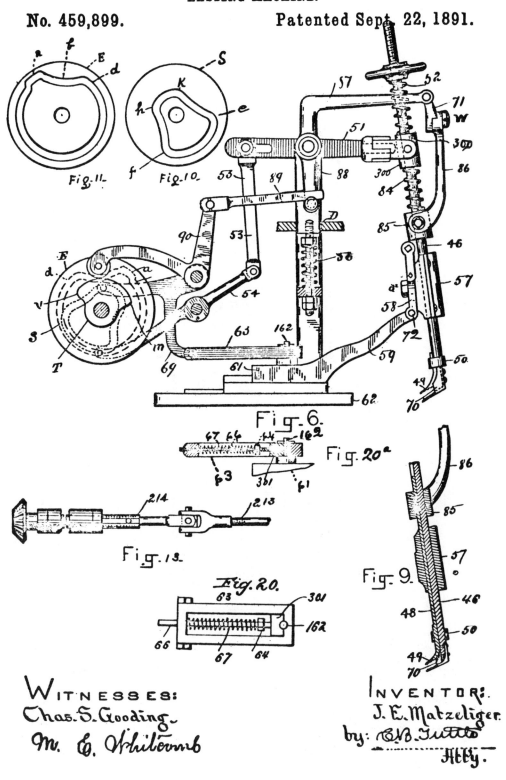

Fig. 11.   Fig. 10.

Fig. 6.

Fig. 20ᵃ

Fig. 13.

Fig. 20.

Fig. 9.

WITNESSES:
Chas. S. Gooding
M. E. Whitcomb

INVENTOR:
J. E. Matzeliger
by: C. B. Tuttle
Att'y.

(No Model.)   10 Sheets—Sheet 6.

J. E. MATZELIGER, Dec'd.
G. W. MOULTON, EXECUTOR.
LASTING MACHINE.

No. 459,899.   Patented Sept. 22, 1891.

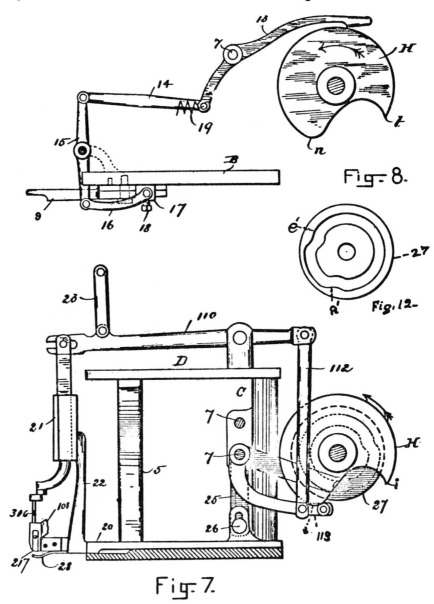

Fig. 8.

Fig. 12.

Fig. 7.

WITNESSES:
Chas. S. Gooding.
M. E. Whitcomb

INVENTOR:
J. E. Matzeliger.
by: C. B. Tuttle
        Atty.

(No Model.)   10 Sheets—Sheet 7.

J. E. MATZELIGER, Deo'd.
G. W. HOULTON, EXECUTOR,
LASTING MACHINE.

No. 459,899.   Patented Sept. 22, 1891.

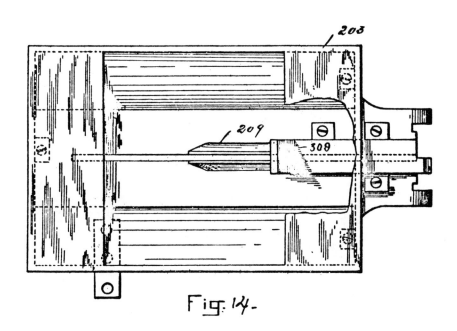

Fig. 14.

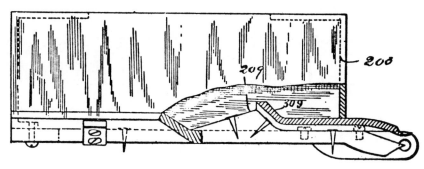

Fig. 15.

WITNESSES:
Chas. S. Gooding.
M. E. Whitcomb

INVENTOR:
J. E. Matzeliger.
by: B. B. Tuttle
Atty.

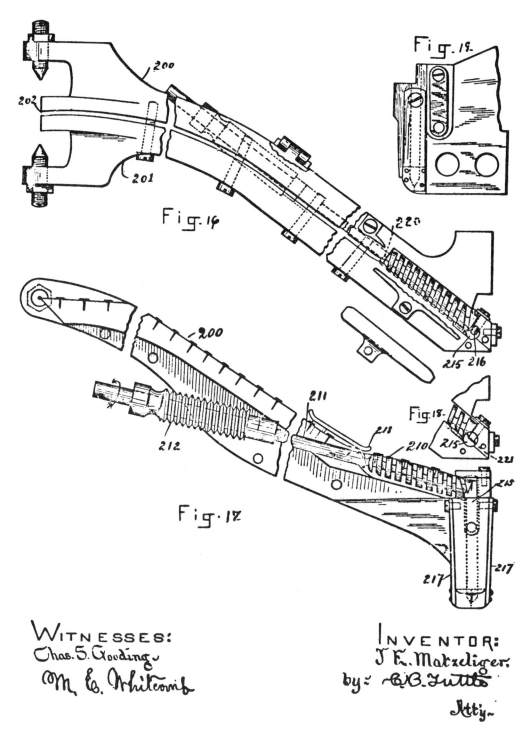

(No Model.)

10 Sheets—Sheet 8.

J. E. MATZELIGER, Dec'd.
G. W. MOULTON, EXECUTOR.
LASTING MACHINE.

No. 459,899.

Patented Sept. 22, 1891.

Fig. 19.

Fig. 16.

Fig. 17.

Fig. 18.

WITNESSES:
Chas. S. Gooding
M. E. Whitcomb

INVENTOR:
J. E. Matzeliger.
by C. B. Tuttle
Atty.

(No Model.)   10 Sheets—Sheet 9.

J. E. MATZELIGER, Dec'd.
G. W. MOULTON, EXECUTOR,
LASTING MACHINE.

No. 459,899.   Patented Sept. 22, 1891.

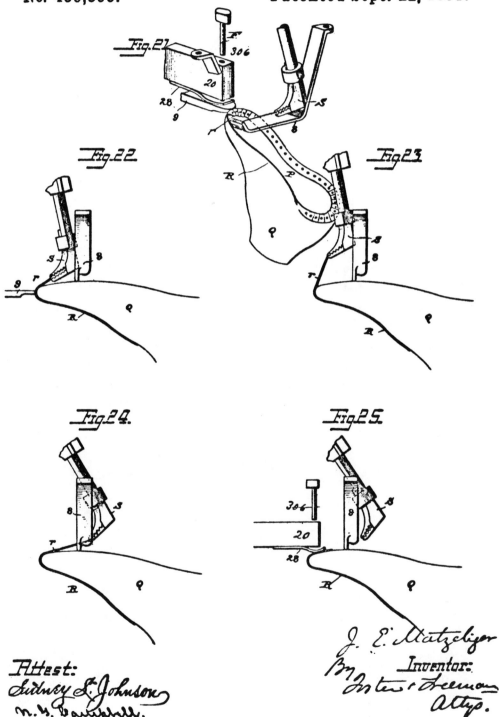

(No Model.) 10 Sheets—Sheet 10.

J. E. MATZELIGER, Dec'd.

G. W. MOULTON, EXECUTOR.

LASTING MACHINE.

No. 459,899. Patented Sept. 22, 1891.

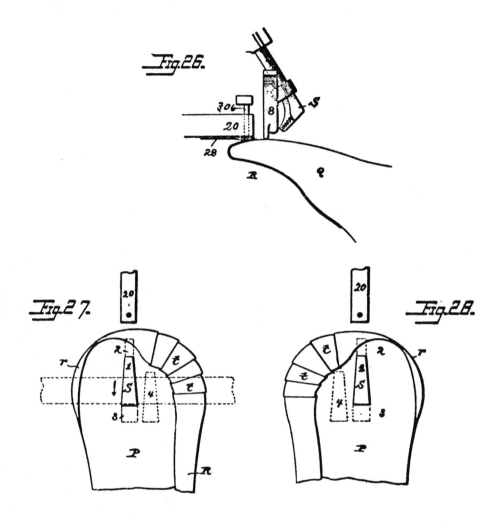

Fig.26.
306
8
S
20
28
R
Q

Fig.27.
Fig.28.
20
20
P
P
R
S
S

Attest:
Sidney L. Johnson
N. H. Campbell.

J. E. Matzeliger
Inventor:
By Foster & Freeman
Attys.

United States Patent Office.

JAN E. MATZELIGER, OF LYNN, MASSACHUSETTS, ASSIGNOR, BY MESNE ASSIGNMENTS, TO THE CONSOLIDATED HAND METHOD LASTING MACHINE COMPANY, OF NASHUA, NEW HAMPSHIRE; GEORGE W. MOULTON EXECUTOR OF JAN E. MATZELIGER, DECEASED.

LASTING-MACHINE.

SPECIFICATION forming part of Letters Patent No. 459,899, dated September 22, 1891.

Application filed August 14, 1885. Serial No. 174,378. (No model.)

To all whom it may concern:

Be it known that I, JAN EARNST MATZELIGER, of Lynn, in the county of Essex and Commonwealth of Massachusetts, have invented certain Improvements in Lasting Shoes, of which the following, taken in connection with the accompanying drawings, is a specification.

This invention relates to lasting shoes and mechanism therefor, and as an aid to more fully understanding certain details of the mechanism employed reference will be made to Letters Patent of the United States, No. 274,207, which have been previously granted to me.

Referring to the drawings, Figure 1 is a side elevation of right side upper part of the machine. Fig. 2 is the reverse of Fig. 1. Fig. 3 is a front elevation of the upper part of the machine. Fig. 4 is a perspective view showing the bottom part of the machine, also the mechanism for giving the plaiting operation to the pincher mechanism. Fig. 5 is a detail. Fig. 6 is a side elevation of the pincher's driving mechanism detached from the other parts of the machine. Fig. 7 is a similar view of the tack or nail driving mechanism and its connections. Fig. 8 is a detail. Fig. 9 is a vertical longitudinal section of the pinchers. Figs. 10, 11, and 12 are cams to be referred to and described hereinafter. Fig. 13 is a detail. Fig. 14 is a plan view of the tack-distributer. Fig. 15 is a vertical longitudinal section thereof. Fig. 16 is a plan view of the channel for carrying tacks to the driver and its connections. Fig. 17 is a side view of Fig. 16 with one side of the channel removed. Figs. 18 and 19 are details. Fig. 20 is a detail plan. Fig. 20ª is a vertical sectional view. Fig. 21 is a perspective view, and Figs. 22 to 28 are diagrams illustrating the progressive operations in the lasting of a shoe.

Before proceeding to describe the constructions in detail of the various parts of my improved lasting-machine I will first refer to the main operating parts which act more directly on the lasted upper and the operations of these parts, and will thereafter describe their particular construction and the devices which are illustrated in the drawings for effecting their operations, which construction and devices may of course be considerably varied without departing from the main features of my invention.

The material to be operated upon is arranged upon a last, as usual—that is, there is a sole P, Fig. 21, tacked to the last Q, and an upper R placed upon the last, with its edge r extending above the same in position to be turned down and tacked to the last, as in the ordinary operation of lasting.

Hereinafter in referring to the presentation of the last to the operating devices I shall for convenience include in the term "last" the last with the material supported thereby.

For seizing the edge of the upper and drawing it down upon the last in proper position to receive the tack I employ a pair of jaws or grippers or tongues S, which I designate by the term "pinchers," and which can be opened to receive the edge r of the upper and then closed upon the same to grip it properly to draw it back.

Heretofore it has been common in lasting shoes to support and feed the last by means of an automatically-operating jack; but this has proved in most cases to be ineffectual because of the differences in the qualities of leather and because of slight variations in the arrangement of the uppers upon the last, so that the operations which would serve to properly stretch one upper and secure it to the sole would not be available in securing the proper result with another upper. For these reasons I support and feed the last by the hands of the operator, who can thereby manipulate the last so as to vary the operations as required by the varying character of the work. As it would not be practicable for the operator to so support the last in his hands as to properly resist the upper and lateral drawing action of the pinchers and so as to gage it in relation to the pinchers, I employ a fixed rest 8 in such a position as to afford a bearing for the bottom of the last, and which is preferably provided with a pointed or sharpened edge which will penetrate the sole upon the last, upon which bearing the last may be turned and adjusted with the

2   459,899

greatest facility, but upon which it may be pressed, so as to prevent any slipping of the last under the draft of the pinchers.

In order to gage the last and adjust it with facility in its exact position to present the edge of the upper to the pinchers that it may be with certainty seized thereby, I employ a gage 9, which remains stationary in proper position to define the position of the last prior to the advance of the pinchers, and I prefer to combine with this gage 9 means whereby it may be withdrawn after the upper has been seized.

In connection with the above-described device I also employ a "wiper" 28, which may be a plate or blade, preferably having some elasticity, which advances over the edge of the last and wipes down and presses back the edge of the upper onto the face of the sole as the pinchers draw back, and which wiper, after the pinchers let go their hold upon the edge of the upper, retains the latter firmly down upon the sole and holds it in position to receive the nail, which is then driven into it to secure it to the sole, after which the wiper returns to its first position prior to the succeeding action of the pinchers upon another portion of the upper.

The general arrangement of the parts above described is illustrated in perspective in Fig. 21, and the successive operations in drawing and securing the upper are illustrated in the diagrams Figs. 22, 23, 24, 25, 26, 27, and 28.

Diagram Fig. 22 shows the last as it is applied to the bearing or rest 8 and against the gage 9 and the pinchers S in the position they occupy after they have advanced and seized the edge of the upper. The pinchers then rise and stretch the upper, as illustrated in diagram Fig. 23, the gage moving back, so as to be out of the way. The pinchers then move forward toward the operator, drawing the upper tightly and nearly to a flat position against the sole, the rest preventing the slipping of the last until the parts are in the position shown in Fig. 24, and as the pinchers reach their forward position the wiper 28, which is shown as in the form of a spring attached to a reciprocating bar, is passed forward in firm contact with the upper and presses it down firmly upon the face of the sole and holds it in position to be secured by a nail, which is driven downward by a driver 306, carried with the bar 20 and wiper. The wiper-bar and driver then move back out of the way, the operator adjusts the last so as to bring another portion of the upper into position to be operated upon, and the above-described operations are repeated. It will be seen that the rest 8 is fixed, as is also the gage 9, during the adjustment of the last in a position, and that the pinchers have a back-and-forth movement, which I will hereinafter designate as the "forward reciprocating movement" of the pinchers, and that they also have a vertical movement for the stretching of the upper and for bringing it down upon the sole.

The forward reciprocating movement of the pinchers is effected by means of a carrier, as I will hereinafter set forth, and in addition to these movements described I also use another carrier which imparts to the pinchers lateral reciprocating movements upon opposite sides of the line of the forward movement for the purpose of folding over or plaiting the edge of the upper, as is requisite in folding it down upon the face of the sole in turning the toe and heel. The movements thus imparted to the pinchers are illustrated in the diagrams Figs. 27 and 28.

In Fig. 27 the upper is represented as having been turned down at the right-hand corner of the last, forming the folds t t, the last bearing upon the rest 8, and the pinchers S are in the position shown in full lines 1. The first movement of the pinchers is backward in the direction of the arrow to the position shown in dotted lines 2, where they seize upon the edge of the upper, and they then ascend and swing forward to the position shown in dotted lines 3, thereby stretching the upper vertically and drawing it forward, after which the pinchers swing to the right to the position shown in dotted lines 4 and descend close to the sole, thereby folding or plaiting the portion of the leather over toward the right, after which the wiper 28 moves forward and presses down the fold close against the sole in position to receive the nail, which is then driven through the fold to secure it. The operator then adjusts the last by turning it upon its bearing 8, and the operations are repeated upon another portion of the upper.

In Fig. 28 the upper is shown as having been plaited over to the left portion of the last. In this case the remaining portion at the toe is folded over by a like series of operations, as before described, on reference to diagram Fig. 27, excepting that after the pinchers move forward and seize the upper and stretch it and draw it back they move to the left to the position shown at 4, thereby making the fold or plait to the left prior to the driving of the nail. It will be seen that these operations are required only upon a portion of the last—that is, where there are corners to be turned—and it is therefore requisite to provide means whereby the operator may at will impart to the pinchers the lateral movements in either direction and arrest such movements. For this purpose I employ any suitable appliances between the driving-shaft and the pinchers in connection with a shifter or device against which the operator may bear by hand or otherwise, so as to at will throw the lateral carrier into and out of operation upon the pinchers, the particular appliances which I have found desirable for this purpose being hereinafter fully set forth, and illustrated in the drawings, the mechanism of which I will now proceed to describe in detail.

All the working mechanism is mounted upon a column A, which stands upon the floor. This column is bent forward and upon its upper end supports a plate B, having in the rear part fixed posts C C, to which is fixed an upper plate D. On the rear of these parts are brackets 2, in which is journaled the main driving-shaft 3. On the end of said driving-shaft is the main drive-wheel 5, and connected with this drive-wheel is an ordinary clutch mechanism having a treadle (not shown) extending down to the floor and adapted to be manipulated by the workman to start and stop the machine. On the shaft 3 are set the cams and cam-wheels which give proper motion to the mechanisms, all as hereinafter more fully described. The upper plate D is further supported upon the lower by means of a pedestal-bracket 4. On the front sides of the posts C are projections 6 6, in which are supported rods 7 7, on which the various bell-crank levers turn.

In order that the upper may be presented properly in position while the pinchers are drawing and stretching the same, the rest 8, which is secured by suitable connections to the plate B or other support, is arranged to afford a bearing below the travel of the pinchers, Figs. 1, 2, and 3. The last is pressed firmly upward against this rest, the bottom of the last bearing against the bottom face of the rest, and is thus prevented from being moved about by the strain on the upper. The position of the rest is such that the last, when held up against the same, as stated, will be in position for the pinchers to come forward and clamp the edge of the upper, as referred to hereinafter.

In proceeding to further describe the machine I shall commence with the gripping devices, by means of which the edge of the upper is seized, drawn over the edge of the last, and held down upon the bottom in position to receive the tacks, and which also at the heel and toe perform the proper plaiting. The pinchers are provided with two jaws, one fixed and the other movable in relation to the fixed jaw. The shank or rod of the pinchers is shown in position in Figs. 1, 2, 3, and 4 at 46, and Fig. 9 is a vertical longitudinal section thereof. Reference may also be had, if desired, to Figs. 11 and 12 of the above-mentioned Letters Patent No. 274,207, where a construction of the pinchers has been fully shown and previously described, said pinchers having laterally-projecting jaws movable one to and from the other. The shank 46 carries the outer or fixed jaw 47. The shank 46 is grooved longitudinally, (see Fig. 9,) and in this groove lies the shank 48 of the movable jaw 49. The shank 48 is held to the shank 46 by means of a collar 50, which collar is fixed to the shank 46, but allows the necessary vertical movement of the shank 48. The vertical movements of the pinchers are imparted by means of a lifter K, which may be constructed in different ways to effect this result. As shown, the lifter is a lever 51, and the main shank 46 of the pinchers is rounded and threaded upon its upper end, as shown in Figs. 1, 2, 3, and 6, and is supported upon the lever 51, which is pivoted upon a standard 88 (see Fig. 6) on the upper plate D. The front end of this lever is forked; the forked portion being arranged to turn on the main portion as a sleeve, and within this fork is located a ring or collar 300, mounted upon trunnions. Through this ring passes the threaded end of the shank 46 aforesaid. The upper end is surrounded by a coil-spring 52, the lower end of which bears upon the ring and the upper end against a thumb-screw, by means of which the tension is regulated. Thus the whole pincher-shank and pinchers are supported upon the collar through the spring 52, and this gives a yielding or spring tension to the pinchers when they have seized the edge of the leather and are drawn up by action of the lever 51. The rear end of the lever 51 is connected by means of a rod 53 to a lever 54, which is pivoted upon the lower rod 7. Its rear end extends back by the side of the cam-wheel E, and a pin in said lever enters the groove in the side of said cam-wheel. The groove in this wheel has a shape as represented in Fig. 11. In order to understand the vertical movement of the pinchers imparted thereto by this cam-wheel, it may here be stated that during this vertical movement, by means of mechanism hereinafter described, the pinchers receive also a movement from and toward the front in order to draw the leather over the last after they have gripped it. We will suppose the pinchers to have gripped the leather. This occurs when the highest part of the cam (marked a, Fig. 11) bears upon the pin of the lever 54, and consequently the pinchers are at their lowest point of depression. At that time they are moved by the other mechanism hereinafter described farthest to the rear. Then from the point a to the point b the pin is made to rise quickly, and thereby the pinchers rise quickly by the same motion, drawing up the leather vertically in order to stretch it upward. From the point b to the point d, as the wheel advances, the pin and rear end of the lever are depressed, and with them the pinchers come down upon the last, having by other mechanism been moved forward over the last; but they do not at first come down as low as they were carried by the point a, since the point d is a less distance from the center of the wheel or shaft, but from the point d round again to the point a, as the wheel advances, the pin of the lever is held downward, and consequently the pinchers are also held down; but it will be apparent from the shape of the groove that the pinchers will be gradually lowered more and more as the pin approaches the point a. During the first part of its movement the pinchers have hold of the leather, and during the latter part of the movement from d to a the jaws of the pinchers have opened and the pinchers have been moved to the rear while being thus lowered

Black Inventors of America

4 **459,899**

in order to bring them again to the leather to take a new grip. Then at the point *a* the pinchers again seize the leather and rise as before. The spring-tension of the pinchers
5 is caused in the lifting part of the movement of the pinchers by the spring 52. As the lever rises, this spring becomes compressed and the tension increases.

In order to guard against any excessive
10 strain and consequent tearing of the leather, I provide a second tension, which may come into play when the spring 52 has reached a certain point of compression. This consists in making the post 88, on which the lever 51
15 is pivoted, rest upon a spring 56, which is supported in the upper part of the bracket 4, heretofore referred to. The post passes through the upper plate and through the pedestal-bracket, and is provided with a collar,
20 threaded upon the post, for adjustment, the spring resting upon the pedestal-bracket. The spring is set at the proper tension—say at a certain number of pounds—depending upon the position of the fulcrum of the lever
25 51 and the limit of tension required. When the strain upon the spring 52 reaches that limit, the spring 56 will yield and thus limit the movement of or strain on the leather.

I have in the description of the parts last
30 given referred to a forward movement of the pinchers, which takes place during the vertical movement, and thus secures a resultant force, causing the pinchers to draw up the leather and carry it over and lay it down
35 upon the last. This forward and the return movements of the pinchers are effected by a carrier J, which may be constructed and operated in different ways. As shown, it is connected with a guide-block 57. The shank of
40 the pinchers below its pivot in the arm 51 passes through the guide-block 57, which block 57 is pivoted to an armed plate 58, and this plate 58 is supported upon the prongs 59, Figs. 1, 2, and 6, but omitted from Fig. 3, which form
45 part of the carrier J, and which embrace the plate on each side and support it by means of small trunnions 72, the trunnions being fixed to the lower corners of the plate. The prongs 59 are carried upon the front end of a block
50 61, sliding on guides on the upper surface of the lower plate B. A slotted bar 63, Figs. 6 and 20, is connected to a bell-crank lever 69, which gives positive movement to the bar and a forward movement to the block 61 through
55 an intermediate tension-spring. From the block 61 projects upward a pin 162. The slot of the bar 63 receives said pin and above a sliding bearing 301, between which and the end of the bar the pin extends. In rear of
60 the pin 162 is a collar 64 on a spindle 66, Fig. 20. This spindle passes back through the rear cross-piece of the bar 63, and between said cross-piece and the collar on said spindle is a coiled spring 67, encircling the spin-
65 dle and tending constantly to press the block 301 forward, so that when a forward pressure is applied by means of the bell-crank lever

upon the bar it applies a yielding pressure through the spring 67 upon the pin 162, and thereby carries forward the carrier J with a
70 yielding pressure, and with it the guide 57 and the pinchers. This, it will be understood, is the force applied to the pinchers to draw the upper to the front over the last. The collar 64 on the spindle 66 in front of the
75 spring is a threaded nut, and by turning it the tension of the spring 67 may be adjusted in order to put a proper amount of strain upon the upper. The pin of the lever 69 works in a groove in the face of the cam S.
80 The shape of this groove is shown in Fig. 10. The rear arm of the bell-crank lever 69 is over the shaft, as shown in the drawings. When the rear end of the lever 69 is up, the pinchers, through the described intermediate
85 connections, are drawn back to take a fresh hold upon the leather, and as the rear arm of said lever 69 comes down the pinchers are carried forward. That part of the cam-groove in wheel S between *e* and *f* holds the pin in one
90 direction or position, during which time the pinchers are in their rear position, and the mechanisms operate to cause them to grasp the edge of the leather. From the points *f* to *h* on the cam S the pin of lever 69 is depressed,
95 and the pinchers, having by that time seized the leather, are carried forward to draw the leather over the last. From *h* to *k* the pin passes round the curve, remaining in position. During this time the pin has no vertical move-
100 ment and the pinchers remain in their advanced position over the last, holding the leather in place. From *k* to *e* the pinchers are drawn back to take a new hold upon the leather.
105 In order that the shoe may be held in position for the pinchers to take hold of the upper, I provide, as above stated, a gage or guide-foot 9. This guide-foot 9 is a bar arranged to slide in suitable ways on the under
110 side of the plate B. It is connected by a series of levers to a cam-wheel H. Fig. 8 of the drawings is a side elevation of these parts— *i. e.*, the cam-wheel H, the bottom plate B, the gage 9, and the mechanism through which
115 motion is transmitted from the cam H to the gage—said parts being detached from the machine. The cam H, it will be understood, is fixed upon the main shaft 3. The lever 13 is pivoted on the top rod 7 and bears one end on
120 the periphery of the cam-wheel H. Its opposite end connects by a rod 14 to the lever 15, which is pivoted on a suitable bracket extending from the plate B upward. The bottom end of this lever 15 connects by a link
125 16, as shown, with a block 17. The block 17 is on the rear end of the gage 9 and is adjustable thereon by means of a set-screw 18. The rear end of lever 13 bears upon the periphery of the cam H, being held thereon by
130 a coiled spring 19. Said spring is secured at one end to the lever, as shown, and one end to the pedestal-bracket 4. When the end of lever 13 reaches the point *n* on the cam-wheel

72

H, it is lifted, and thereby moves forward the gage 9, and during the movement of the lever from the point n to the point t on the cam the end of the lever remains lifted, and con-
5 sequently the gage 9 is held forward. During the time the gurde or bearing 9 is stationary and the shoe is pressed, as before described, against the extreme end of said bearing the pinchers advance and take hold of
10 the edge of the upper. At the point t on the cam H the rear end of the lever is depressed. The gage is thereby drawn backward and is held backward while the lever passes from the point t to the point n on the cam. Dur-
15 ing this time the pinchers move upward and forward, as before described, to stretch and pull the upper over the last, the foot being now withdrawn from contact with the upper. At the point n the end of the lever is again
20 lifted and the movements of the guide-foot repeated.

I shall now proceed to describe the mechanism for opening and closing the jaws of the pinchers for gripping and releasing the edge
25 of the leather.

It will be borne in mind from the description heretofore given of the general movement of the pinchers that they pass backward from the last, gradually descending dur-
30 ing such backward movement. This brings the pinchers back against the edge of the upper, and it is necessary at that point that the movable jaw should be raised, so that the gripping-face of the fixed jaw should pass be-
35 neath the inturned portion of the leather. It will be observed that the jaws are opened back to the rear, as shown in Fig. 9, so that when the movable jaw is raised it opens the space between the two jaws. In practice it
40 is necessary that the upper jaw should be raised about three-fourths of an inch, and this occurs just before the jaw comes back against the upper. The position of these jaws is shown clearly in Fig. 9. The edge of
45 the upper extends upward and forward to enter the pinchers as they descend open. The fixed jaw of the pinchers is provided with side guards or fenders 70, which prevent the upper from entering too far into the pinchers.
50 The fixed jaw is secured to the shank 46 by screws, and is therefore detachable from the shank. The movable jaw is raised by means of a cam on the main shaft through intermediate links and levers and is forced down by
55 a spring 84. The upper end of the shank 48 is connected to a collar 85, which surrounds the shank 46 and slides freely thereon. A forked rod 86 is connected by an intermediate link 71 to a bell-crank lever 87. The link 71
60 is pivoted one end to the forked rod 86 and one end to the lever 87, as shown. This is done to permit a side movement of the pinchers, referred to hereinafter. The lower or forked end of the rod 86 embraces the collar
65 85, to which it is pivoted, as shown in Fig. 6. The bell-crank lever 87 is pivoted upon the standard 88 and is preferably forked at its

upper end to pass the main shaft of the pinchers. The vertical arm of the bell-crank le-
70 ver is connected by a pusher-bar 89 to the bell-crank lever 90, which bears on the cam T. (See Fig. 6.) The shape and position of this cam are such as to throw up the rear end of the bell-crank lever and advance the
75 pusher to lift the movable jaw immediately after the nailer advances and just before the advance movement of the nailer is completed. It begins to open at the rise of the cam T at the point m on the cam. The first move-
80 ment is sufficient to cause the jaws to release the leather, and this occurs just before the nailer, and consequently the presser-foot, hereinafter described, reaches its extreme forward movement. The increased rise of
85 the cam from m to v continues to lift the jaw until at the point v it is at its greatest height. The lifting of this jaw takes place during the backward movement of the pinchers, and immediately after the fixed jaw reaches the
90 edge of the leather the rear end of the bell-crank lever 90 drops from the point of the cam T, and the movable jaw is forced down by the spring 84 to grip the upper and remains constantly in contact with the leather until
95 lifted by the movement of the cam and intermediate mechanism.

Only the movements of the pincher mechanism heretofore described are necessary in operating on the upper at the sides of the last.
100 In order to form plaiting at the heel and toe and occasionally at other points, the lateral movement before referred to is required, and it is also necessary that in such movement the pinchers should be adapted to
105 yield to prevent tearing the upper. In order to permit of lateral movement, I make the forked end of lever 51 in the form of a sleeve to turn on the end of the lever. I also join the arm 86 to its support, forming the joint at W,
110 as before described; also, the trunnions 72 are extended, as shown in Fig. 3, and are allowed to slide loosely in the bearings of the prongs 59, (see Fig. 2,) whereby they are supported, and the plate 58 is also pivoted to the plate
115 57 by a pivot-pin a². The lateral movement is effected by means of the laterally-reciprocating carrier 40, which, as shown, is a bar or pin, but may be constructed in different ways and so connected with the pinchers as to
120 carry them with it. As shown, the carrier-bar 40 is employed in connection with a horizontal rod 73, which is arranged in rear of the pincher-shanks, as shown, and which is reciprocated longitudinally by the movements
125 of said carrier-rod 40. On the rod 73 are two coiled springs 74 74, bearing their inner or contiguous ends against a pin or collar 304, Figs. 3 and 4, fixed in or on the rod. The outer ends of these springs bear, respectively,
130 against the collars 75 76, provided with downward extensions 77 and horizontal extensions 78. The horizontal extensions 78 are fitted to a groove in the plate or block 57, which supports the extensions and collars, and con-

6   **459,899**

sequently the rod 73. The collars are loose on the rod 73, and screws 79, passing from the extensions 77 into the block 57, serve as means whereby to adjust the collars toward
5 and from each other on the rod, and thus to regulate the tension of the springs 74. The opposing powers of the springs 74 operate to keep the block 57 and pincher-shanks supported thereby midway between the collars
10 75 76, so that a movement of the rod 73 to the left, for example, applies a yielding force to carry the pinchers in that direction. A reverse movement of the rod to the right will in like manner carry the pinchers in that di-
15 rection. This force is applied through the rods 40 and 73 and through the springs 74 and the collars 75 76. The power which carries the pinchers to either side is limited by the tension of the springs 74, and this, it will be
20 understood, is the force applied to stretch the upper in this direction, whether for purposes of plaiting or otherwise.

It will be understood that the pinchers always return to the center point or line to
25 grasp the upper, and the movement in plaiting is from that point outward in an oblique line. The springs 74 will yield sufficiently to accommodate this movement. This yielding lateral movement of the pinchers is not abso-
30 lutely necessary for lasting, nor is it required at all times; but it is very advantageous, and especially for operating about the toe and shank. It is desirable, therefore, to leave the mechanism whereby the lateral movements
35 are effected subject to the control of the operator, in order that he may put it into operation at the time desired. To this end I have provided mechanism as follows, (shown in Fig. 4:) The arm 94 carries the pin 40, which
40 enters a slot in the head 303 of the rod 73, and by varying the position and extent of vibration of the arm 94 or of the carrier the requisite changes in the lateral movements of the pinchers may be effected. To vary these
45 movements I employ a driver M, constituting part of the connections between the main driving-shaft and the lateral carrier and connected with the shifter. This driver is shown as a sliding block 99, mounted on a vibrating
50 bar 100. An arm 96 is fixed to the arm 94 and extends laterally therefrom. It is provided with a slotted head 97, and in this slot in this head projects a pin 98, fixed in the block 99, which slides on the bar 100, which
55 bar 100 is pivoted upon an arm 101 on the plate D. The outer side of the arm 101 is provided with an arm 102, which is connected by means of a bar 103 to the bell-crank lever 104. This lever and its operating-cam are
60 fully shown in Fig. 5. This bell-crank lever 104 has a pin which enters a cam-groove in the periphery of the wheel X on the main shaft. It will be apparent that when the lever is rocked it will impart longitudinal move-
65 ment to the bar 103 and vibrate the bar 100 either to the right or left, and the block acts upon the slotted head 97 of the arm 96 through

the pin 98. It will be plain that lateral action both in direction and amount upon the arm
70 94 will depend upon the position of the pin 98. If the pin be in the center of the slot in the end of the arm 96, it will have no effect upon the arm 94, but the bar 100 will simply turn. If, however, the pin 98 be drawn into
75 the front end of the slot and the connecting-rod 103 be pushed to the front, the pin 98 will act upon the head 97 as upon a lever and will push the rod 73 in one direction and carry the pinchers to the right; but if the pin 98 is
80 in the other end of the slot a like movement of the connecting-rod 103 will draw the rod 73 in the opposite direction and carry the pinchers to the left. The object of this twofold graduated motion is to draw and plait the up-
85 per at one time in one direction and at another time in some other direction and to vary the extent of the draft.

It is desirable, as before stated, that this mechanism should be subjected to the con-
90 trol of the workman, so as to be thrown into or out of operation at any moment. To this end I use a shifter N in connection with mechanism as follows, (also shown in Fig. 4:) A lever 105 is pivoted upon a bracket upon the
9_ machine. This lever is connected at its lower end by a connecting-rod 107 to a shifter in the form of a bell-crank lever 108. The lever 108 is pivoted on a bracket 109 upon the machine and is forked at one end to receive the
100 knee of the operator. On the bracket 109 is a cross-bar 110, provided with leaf-springs 111. Said springs reach over and bear upon the lever 108 to hold it in place. The upper end of lever 105 is connected by a rod 106
105 to the block 99, which carries the pin 98. It will be apparent that when the lever 108 stands in the center of cross-bar 110, as in Fig. 4, the pin 98 is at the center of the slot in the head of arm 96. The pinchers will then
110 consequently have no lateral movement. When the lever 108 is pushed to either side, it will draw the pin 98 into one end of the slot and the pinchers will commence to move in a side line, as before described. The le-
115 ver 108 is intended and arranged to be moved by the knee of the operator. The shifter is retained in position when set by the force of the springs 111. I am aware that this lever could be arranged to be operated by the foot
120 or other part of the body, though I believe the arrangement shown herein to be the most convenient.

I now proceed to describe the tacking and nailing mechanism. The tacks are brought
125 to the driving-point by polished steel guides, Figs. 16 to 19, forming a channel 202, leading from the tack-distributer, hereinafter explained, to a point just below the driver. The forward ends of the guides are supported upon
130 the forward end of a sliding bar 20, Fig. 1. This bar is arranged to slide in a suitable channel in the block 62, Fig. 7. The extreme end of the guide-channel turns down vertically and in line with the driver 306. The driver

slides in a guide-block 21, Fig. 7, which is supported by a vertical post 22, fixed upon the bar 20. The upper end of the driver (see Fig. 7) is connected to a lever 110, the forked end of the lever receiving the pin at the upper end of the driver. The lever 110 is supported in a post on the plate D and is connected by a link 23 to the bottom end of a rod 34, Fig. 1. The link 23 is pivoted both to the driver and to the rod 34. The bottom end of the rod 34 is enlarged to slide freely in the inner bore of a hollow post 35, fixed upon the plate D. The rod 34 is surrounded by a coiled spring 36, which bears one end against the head on the rod and the other against a collar 37 on the top end of the rod. The collar 37 is a threaded nut arranged to turn on the rod, and thus the tension of the spring may be regulated. This spring, it will be understood, is the force that drives the hammer down to insert the tack. On the collar 37 is a check-nut 38, whereby the collar may be fastened when once adjusted. Under the bottom end of the rod 34 is a spring 307 to prevent the hammer from descending too far and reduce impact. This spring sets upon the plate D within the hollow post. Instead of the spring some fibrous material, as leather or rubber, may be used. The rear end of lever 110 is connected by a connecting-rod 112 to a lever pivoted upon the lower rod 7, which has a transverse pin under the cam H, Fig. 7. This cam is constructed, as shown, to depress the end of rod 113 and thereby to elevate the driver through the described intermediate connections and hold the driver lifted until the rod reaches the point i on cam H. At this point the rod is suddenly released, thereby allowing the hammer to descend, and it is forced instantly downward by the spring 36, delivering a blow upon the head of the tack. The rear end of the bar 20 is turned slightly upward and is connected by means of a pin 26, Fig. 7, to one end of the bell-crank lever 25. The other end of the bell-crank lever carries a transverse pin that enters a cam-groove in the face of wheels 27, Fig. 7. The shape of this cam-groove is shown in Fig. 12. When the rear end of the lever 25 is raised, the bar 20 and consequently the tack-driving mechanism are pushed forward, and when the lever is depressed this mechanism is drawn back. That part of the cam-groove from a' to e' holds the lever down, during which time the bar 20 is held back and the pinchers come forward and grasp and draw the upper over the last. At the point e' the end of lever 25 is depressed. The bar 20 is thereby pushed forward, carrying the tacker into position for driving the tack. That part of the cam-groove from e' to a holds the lever depressed. During this time the tack is driven. At the point e' the end of the lever is raised to withdraw the bar 20 and given opportunity for the operation of the pinchers to be repeated. A wiper 28, preferably in the form of a spring, is secured at one end to the forward under side of bar 20, and the outer end of this wiper extends forward under the bar in a curved line, as shown in Fig. 7. This wiper extends under the tack-hammer, and when the bar 20 is pushed forward, as before described, the wiper bears upon the upper to fold it over the edge of the last and hold it in place while the tack is driven. I attach great importance to this wiper, and it may be operated in different ways and independently of the tack-guide. It advances forward in line with the draw of the pinchers and acts very much like the thumb of the hand when drawn over the edge of the strained upper to smooth the leather and holds it down closely to the last while the tack is inserted. The wiper, as shown, is attached directly to the bar. It will be evident, however, that it could be operated by an independent mechanism, if desired. The mechanism is so preferably timed that the bar 20 commences to go forward while the pinchers have hold of the upper over the last, and when the wiper 28 comes over the last sufficiently to get a good bearing upon the edge of the upper the pinchers let go and fly back. The tacker-bar 20 continues forward over the last, the wiper 28 now holding and smoothing the upper as it advances until the extreme forward movement of the bar 20 is reached. The arm 113 is then immediately released, as before described, the driver is forced down by the spring 36, and the tack is thereby inserted, it being allowed to pass down through a hole in the guide and wiper. The two steel bars 200 201, which form the guide-channel, are placed adjacent to each other and are held together by screws or other obvious means. These bars are grooved and separated to form the channel 202, which receives the tacks as they come from the distributer. The distributer is a box 203. One end of the box is pivoted to the guide, as shown in Figs. 1 and 8. The free end of the box is raised and lowered by a mechanism as follows: On the main shaft is a pulley, and on a post 205, fixed upon the plate D, is another pulley 204. A belt connects these two pulleys and transmits power from the main shaft to turn the pulley 204. The pulley 204 carries an eccentric-pin 206, that operates in the slotted end of lever 207, pivoted to the post in the plate D, and is connected by a connecting-rod 208 to the free end of the box 203. It will now be understood that each revolution of the wheel 204 operates to raise and lower the free end of the box. The tacks are placed into the box 203 promiscuously in bulk, and as the box lifts and falls the tacks pass by gravity from the free end of the box to the other, and in the bottom of the box a slot is formed that commences near the free end of the box and opens out at the opposite end into the channel 202. This slot is formed by cutting through the bottom of the box and is sufficiently wide to receive the shanks of the tacks, but will not receive the heads of the tacks into the slot. Near the center of the box is formed a ridge

209. Said ridge is formed by raising the sides of the channel at this point, and it is inclined two ways, as shown. (See Fig. 15.) When the box 203 is depressed, so that the tacks fall to the outer end thereof, some of the tacks fall into the slot and there hang suspended by their heads bearing upon the sides of the channel, so that when the box is lifted again the bulk of the tacks pass to the other end of the box, leaving the channel unobstructed and allowing those tacks which hang in the slot to slide forward up the first incline and over the top of the ridge and perhaps down the second incline. The channel in front of this ridge is covered, and all tacks that pass over the ridge are prevented by the ridge from passing back when the box is lowered again. In this manner the tacks are continuously distributed to the channel in front of the ridge and find exit through this channel out of the box. The tacks are moved along the channel by the inclining of the box and the jar of the machine. The box is pivoted to the channel in such manner as to bring the exit from the box in alignment with the groove 202, so that as the tacks exit from the box they pass into the groove 202 and are moved downward by the constant jar of the tack-driver or by other agitating means. At the lower end of the channel 202 is formed a chamber adapted to receive the screw 210. This chamber is formed by enlarging the channel at this point or by arranging the screw adjacent to the channel. This screw receives the tacks from the channel 202, carries them along, and drops them one by one into the guide-tube 215, as designed for use. To this end the screw is provided with a shank or spindle 211, which is journaled to turn in a bushing 212, which is preferably made to screw into a suitable hole in the channel-bars 200 201. A collar on each side or end of the bushing prevents endwise movement of the screw. The rear end of the screw-shank 211 is connected by a universal-joint connection to one end of a connecting-rod 213, Fig. 1. The other end of the rod 213 is connected by a universal joint to the shaft 214. This shaft 214 is journaled to turn in a bracket on the machine-frame and carries a crown-wheel that engages a similar wheel on the main driving-shaft. The result of this mechanism is to give motion to the screw 210, and the mechanism is so timed as to give one revolution of the screw to each complete operation of the tack-driver. Each revolution of the screw drops one tack into the vertical tube 215, where it hangs suspended by the head on a spring-tripper 216, Fig. 16, which is sufficient to retain the tack, but which yields readily to the descent of the driver. Spring-guides 217 guide the tack in its descent directly to the leather.

It remains to be observed that the channel-groove is preferably made wedge shape to prevent the points of the tacks from crowding past each other. It is also covered to prevent the tacks from being thrown out by the jar of the driver. At the point where the tack enters the screw 210 a spring 218 is arranged with its end adapted to press lightly upon the top until it has fairly entered the threads of the screw. The screw 210 at the point where it commences is the size of the shank or spindle and gradually is enlarged to the full size, thus forming a gimlet-like screw-section. This formation allows the screw to take the tack close up under the head, and to this end also a slight lateral angle 220 is here formed in the channel. (See Fig. 16.) The screw is revolved in the direction of the arrow, Fig. 17, and a tack having once entered the screw is carried along regularly between the screw-threads and the side of the channel-point downward until it arrives at or near the extreme end of the screw. Here the angle of the screw-thread changes abruptly to an angle of about forty-five degrees, so that the tack is moved point forward into the guide-tube 215. This special formation of screw causes the tack to turn into the guide-tube point first. It also allows the extreme end of the screw to be notched out at one side at 221. (See Fig. 18.) This allows the screw to be set forward over the guide-tube in order to carry the tack completely into the guide-tube before dropping the same; but a partial revolution of the screw throws the notched part of the screw in line with the tube, leaving a free passage to drop the tack, and thus allowing the driver to descend without striking the screw. The driver should of course be so timed as to lift out of the tube in time to allow the continuous movement of the screw.

I would also call attention to the curvature of the guide-bars 200 201.

I am aware that some articles, as buttons, may be carried from a distributer operated similar to the one herein described through a straight channel; but in transmitting tacks I have encountered great difficulty to keep the tacks in place and prevent them from crowding in the channel. This difficulty arises largely from the inclination imparted to the guide, and to obviate this I have curved the guides, as shown, and this allows the box to be pivoted out of line with the feeding end of the channel. This construction very much reduces the vibration, and the difficulty before encountered is practically obviated.

I do not here claim the tacking mechanism shown and described, as it will form the subject of a separate application for Letters Patent.

I do not here claim the method of lasting herein set forth, as it constitutes the subject of a separate application for Letters Patent, Serial No. 266,028.

Without limiting myself to the precise construction and arrangement of parts shown, I claim—

1. In a lasting-machine, the combination, with a fixed rest, of a single pair of pinchers suspended above said rest, and mechanism for

moving said pinchers vertically and forward and back above and over the rest from a position in front to a position back of the same, substantially as described.

2. In a lasting-machine, the combination, with a fixed rest, of a single pair of pinchers suspended above said rest and adapted to be moved vertically and forward and back above and over the rest from a position in front to a position toward the back of the same, and a forwardly and backwardly moving elastic wiper, substantially as described.

3. A lasting-machine provided with a frame, a rest supported in a fixed position on the frame, a pair of pinchers and appliances supporting them above the rest in position to swing from front to back over the rest, and mechanism connected with the pinchers to open and close and move the same vertically and forward and back, substantially as described.

4. In a lasting-machine, the combination, with a fixed rest having its bearing-surface upon its under side, of a single pair of pinchers suspended above said rest and adapted to be moved vertically, laterally, and forward and back above the horizontal plane of the rest, whereby the upper is drawn over the last and plaited at the same time, substantially as set forth.

5. In a lasting-machine, the combination, with the reciprocating pinchers and fixed rest, of a guide 9, adjustable to and from the rest, for the purpose set forth.

6. In a lasting-machine, the combination, with the reciprocating pinchers, of a rest having an under bearing for the last, and an edge guide 9, movable toward and from the rest, substantially as described.

7. In a lasting-machine, the combination, with the pinchers and last-rest and with the devices for reciprocating the pinchers back and forth, of the devices for reciprocating the pinchers laterally, a shaft from which motion is imparted to said devices through a movable driver, and a shifter whereby said driver may be moved by the operator to vary or arrest the lateral reciprocation, substantially as described.

8. The combination, in a lasting-machine, of pinchers and pincher-actuating mechanism, the driver M, and the shifter N and connections, substantially as described.

9. In a lasting-machine, the combination, with the pinchers of a lasting-machine supported to move freely, of a carrier J and devices for moving it laterally, said carrier connected with said pinchers to swing them sidewise, substantially as described.

10. In a lasting-machine, the combination, with the pinchers, of two carriers 40 J, one moving back and forth and the other from side to side and each connected to operate the pinchers, substantially as described.

11. In a lasting-machine, the combination, with the pinchers, of a laterally-movable carrier, driving-shaft, movable driver, and a shifter arranged in the line of connection between the pinchers and shaft in position to be moved by the operator, substantially as described.

12. In a lasting-machine, the combination, with the pinchers and carrier, of a vibrating block, a bearing movable upon said block past the axis thereof, and a shifter connected with said bearing and arranged to be operated by the attendant, substantially as described.

13. In a lasting-machine, the combination, with the pinchers and the forward and laterally movable carriers therefor, of the driving-shaft and connections between the same and the carriers, and a driver connected with the laterally-reciprocating carrier and adjustable to vary the movements of the carrier, substantially as described.

14. In a lasting-machine, the combination, with the pinchers and devices for moving the same forward and laterally, of a lifter K, provided with a swivel and a sleeve, substantially as described.

15. In a lasting-machine, the combination, with the pinchers S, forward and lateral carriers J and 40, and lifter K, of side spring-bearings interposed between the lateral carrier and the pinchers, substantially as described.

16. In a lasting-machine, the combination of the pinchers S, lateral carrier 40, and intermediate yielding bearings, substantially as described.

17. In a lasting-machine, the combination of the pinchers S, a lifter K, and forward and lateral carriers J and 40, and vertical and lateral yielding bearings between the pinchers and said lifter and carriers, substantially as described.

18. In a lasting-machine, the combination of the vertically-reciprocating lifter provided with a swinging yoke supporting a pivoted ring or collar, in combination with pinchers supported by a shaft extending through said collar, substantially as described.

19. In a lasting-machine, the combination, with the swinging pinchers, of a slide connected with the movable jaw thereof and jointed connections 71 86 between said slide and an operating-shaft, substantially as described.

20. In a lasting-machine, and in combination, pinchers provided with mechanism for causing them to grip the leather and draw it over the last, and a wiper and mechanism, substantially as described, to advance it over the last toward the position of the pinchers, said mechanisms being timed so that the wiper shall commence to advance while the pinchers hold the leather tightly down over the last and continue to advance after the pinchers let go and bear upon and hold the leather tightly stretched during the latter part of the movement, substantially as described.

21. In a lasting-machine, the combination, with the reciprocating pinchers, of a nailer

77

10   459,899

and means, substantially as described, for moving the latter horizontally toward and from the last independently of the movements of the pinchers, substantially as de-
5 scribed.

22. In a lasting-machine, in combination, pinchers provided with mechanism for causing them to grip the leather and draw it over the last, a nailing mechanism, substantially
10 as described, adapted to advance into the position of the pinchers for inserting the tack, and a wiper independent of the pinchers for smoothing and holding the strained upper while the tack is inserted, the wiper being
15 timed to take hold in time for the pinchers to let go and give place to the nailer, all substantially as described.

23. In a lasting-machine, the pinchers suspended as described and provided with a
20 sleeve on a lever 51, joint W, loose trunnions 72, and mechanism to impart a forward lateral movement to the pinchers, substantially as described.

24. In a lasting-machine, the combination
25 of the shank 48 and upper jaw, the shank 46, with lower jaw, collar 85, spring 84, rod 86, link 71, bell-crank lever 87, and connections with the driving mechanisms, substantially as described.
30   25. In a lasting-machine, the combination

of the guide-foot 9, sliding on the under side of plate B, the rod 16, lever 15, and connections with the driving mechanism, substantially as described.

26. In a lasting-machine, the combination 35 of the driver, the guide-block 21, lever 110, the link 23, spring 36, rod 35, post on the plate D, and the driving mechanism connected to the lever 110, substantially as described.

27. In a lasting-machine, in combination 40 with the driver suspended as described, the bar 20, the lever 25, and driving mechanism, substantially as described.

28. The combination, with the stretching devices of a lasting-machine, of a box 203, 45 provided with the described slot or channel and double incline ridgeway 209, with the channel and tack-driver, all substantially as described.

29. In a lasting-machine, the combination, 50 in the pinchers, with the upper movable jaw, of the lower jaw and side flanges secured thereto, whereby the edge of the leather is prevented from entering the pinchers too far, substantially as described.

JAN E. MATZELIGER.

Witnesses:
  G. B. DUNHAM,
  C. B. TUTTLE.

Norman Rillieux

By 1860, there were a quarter of a million free blacks below the Mason-Dixon Line. Fortunately for the sugar industry and all those who have subsequently prospered from it, the father of Norbert Rillieux was born free and became a wealthy engineer.

Rillieux, a very bright and intelligent child, was sent to the best engineering schools in Europe. By the time he was 24, he had published several papers on The Functions and Economic Implications of the Steam Engine. At 25, he was instructor at one of the finest academies in Paris, where he taught Applied Mechanics and published other papers.

Returning to the U.S. in the 1830's, Rillieux set up shop near his father's plantation, on the outskirts of New Orleans. He was intrigued by the possibility of improving the slow primitive sugar refining process, known as the "Jamaica Train." Rillieux would run his fingers through a small bowl of course, brown sugar and find himself thinking, "There has got to be a better way." And not only a *better* way, he decided, but also a *cheaper* way. Norbert Rillieux was a *true son*, indeed, of our tribe of ingenious black inventors.

By 1846, he had developed a process that turned sugar cane into a *finer grade of sugar, at one half the cost*. It had been his earlier preoccupation with the applications of steam, that furnished the clue for an improved method. He perfected a vacuum pan, which revolutionized the sugar industry. The "Rillieux Process" was quickly adopted by Cuban and Mexican sugar refiners and he was soon the most famous engineer in the state of Louisiana. Dr. Charles Brown, sugar chemist of the United States Department of Agriculture, said *"Rillieux's invention is the greatest in the history of american chemical engineering."*

For several years, he turned his attention to the study of archeology and ended up spending ten years deciphering hieroglyphics. Then, Europe realized the value of Rillieux's process and he returned to engineering. He halved the cost of sugar production there and spent the remainder of his life in Europe.

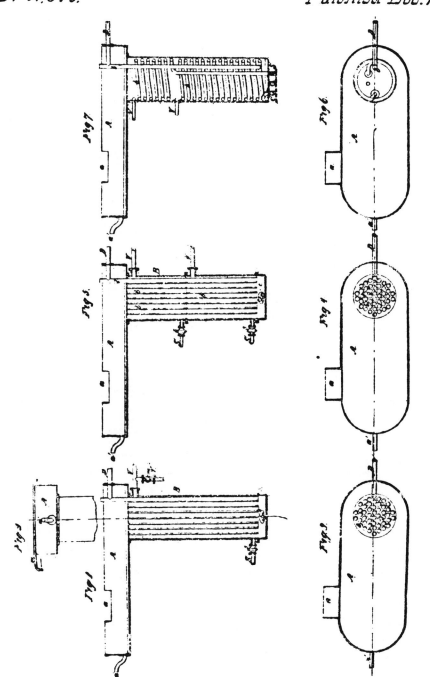

Sheet 1. 4 Sheets

N. Rillieux,

Evaporating Pan,

Nº 4,879.

Patented Dec. 10, 1846.

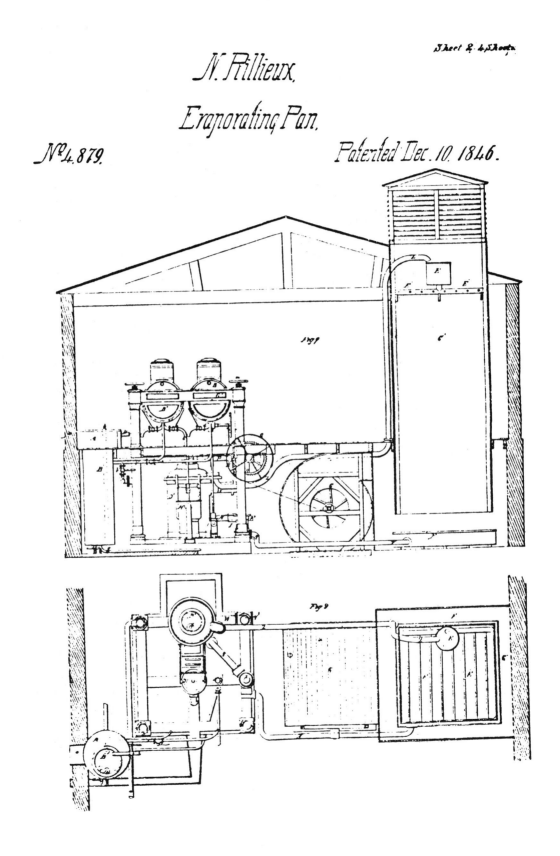

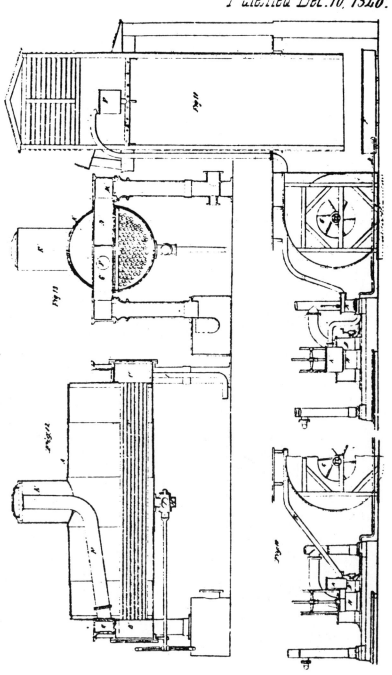

N. Rillieux,

Evaporating Pan.

№ 4.879.

Sheet 3.4 Sheets

Patented Dec. 10. 1846.

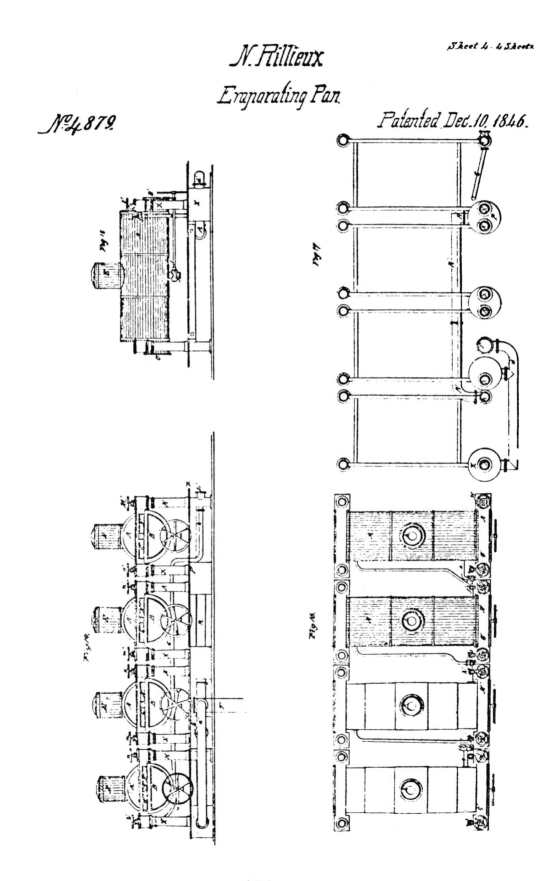

N. Rillieux

Evaporating Pan.

Sheet 4. 4 Sheets

Nº 4879.

Patented Dec. 10. 1846.

United States Patent Office.

NORBERT RILLIEUX, OF NEW ORLEANS, LOUISIANA.

IMPROVEMENT IN SUGAR-MAKING.

Specification forming part of Letters Patent No. **4,879,** dated December 10, 1846.

To all whom it may concern:

Be it known that I, NORBERT RILLIEUX, of New Orleans, in the parish of Orleans and State of Louisiana, have invented new and useful Improvements in the Method of Heating, Evaporating, and Cooling Liquids, especially intended for the manufacture of sugar; and I do hereby declare that the following is a full, clear, and exact description of the principle or character which distinguishes them from all other things before known, and of the manner of making, constructing, and using the same, reference being had to the accompanying drawings, making part of this specification, in which—

Figure 1, Plate 1, is a longitudinal vertical section of the heater; Fig. 2, (same plate,) an end elevation of the upper part, A, thereof; Fig. 3, (same plate,) a plan; Figs. 4 and 5, (same plate,) a plan and vertical section of a modification of the mode of constructing the heater, and Figs. 6 and 7 (same plate) a plan and vertical section of another modification in the mode of construction. Fig. 8, Plate 2, is a plan of the cooler in connection with the entire apparatus, and Fig. 9 (same plate) an elevation of the same; Fig. 10, Plate 3, an elevation of a modification of the entire apparatus represented in Plate 2; and Fig. 11, Plate 3, a vertical section of the apparatus thus modified; Figs. 12 and 13, (same plate,) longitudinal and transverse vertical sections of one of the boilers or pans; Fig. 14, Plate 4, an elevation of a series of evaporating-pans; Fig. 15, (same plate,) a side elevation; Fig. 16, (same plate,) a plan thereof, and Fig. 17 (same plate) a horizontal section taken at the line X X of Fig. 14.

The same letters indicate like parts in all the figures.

My invention consists, first, of a heater for clarifying saccharine juices preparatory to the evaporating process, but which may be employed simply for heating the juice preparatory to clarifying; second, of a cooler employed in connection with the vacuum-pans or evaporators or boiling apparatus, by means of which the saccharine juices are cooled by a current of air that they may be employed as a means of condensation for the vacuum-pans, at the same time preparing them by partial evaporation for the evaporating-pans; and, third, of an arrangement of vacuum-pans or evaporators.

First, of the heater: This part of my invention is distinguished from all other things before known by so arranging it that the saccharine juice is conducted through a tube or pipe and delivered at the bottom of a vessel provided with tubes, through which the juice rises gradually to the top, receiving heat from the tubes which are heated by the circulation of hot water or steam around them, the upper part of the vessel being provided with a rim which has a pipe for the clarified juice to pass off, and a spout for the discharge of the scums which is placed a little above the connection of the pipe that carries off the clarified juice.

Of the cooler: The nature of this part of my invention consists of the employment of a current of air from a fan-blower, which passes up a vertical flume and meets the saccharine juice or other fluid falling in spray from a perforated pan or pipes above, and then in using the saccharine juice thus cooled and partly evaporated for the condensing process by passing it through the pipes of what is known as the "Hall Condenser" to make the vacuum in the pans. After this the juice is separated, a portion, in a partly-heated state, is fed into the first of the series of evaporating-pans, and the rest returned to the cooler preparatory to another operation. By means of this arrangement I attain an economical result, for the cooling operation partly evaporates the saccharine juice, and at the same time avoids the necessity of using water for carrying on the process, which saving is very important on account of the great scarcity of water in many parts of the sugar-growing country.

Of the evaporating-pans: A series of vacuum or partial vacuum pans have been so combined together as to make use of the vapor from the evaporation of the juice in the first to heat the juice in the second, and the vapor from this to heat the juice in the third, which latter is in connection with a condenser, the degree of pressure in each successive one being less; but the defect in this plan is that when the last, called the "striking-pan," (so called from the fact that the sugar is there reduced to the condition in which it is to be transferred to the coolers or granulating-vats,) is stopped, all the others in the series must be stopped also, and as this occurs every time the striking-pan is discharged and when it is used for reboiling the molasses it becomes a serious inconvenience. The object of my improvement is to avoid this inconvenience by connecting the striking-pan by a pipe governed with a cock with the first sirup-pan, so as to heat it with the vapor from the said first sirup-pan, so that the connection can be closed at pleasure without interrupting the operation of the series of sirup-pans, the last of which is in connection with the condenser, instead of being in connection with the striking-pan. The number of sirup-pans may be increased or decreased at pleasure so long as the last of this series is in connection with the condenser, and it will be obvious that the striking-pan, instead of being heated with steam from the first sirup-pan, may be heated by vapor from either of the series except the last, although I prefer to take the vapor from the first; but this connection must be independent of the connection between the several sirup-pans with each other and that of the last of the series with the condenser.

In the accompanying drawings, Plate 1, A is the trough of the heater at the top of a vertical cylindrical vessel, B, containing a series of vertical tubes, b, the upper ends of which are attached to and open into the trough A, and their lower ends attached to a perforated plate near the bottom of and opening into a chamber, c, at the bottom of the vessel B, provided with a man-hole, c', for the purpose of cleaning out. One of the vertical tubes b extends up higher than the rest, and communicates with a pipe, D, through which the saccharine juice is introduced from the coarse strainers (in the usual manner) that separate the coarse impurities. The juice passes down this tube to the chamber c, and gradually rises in the tubes b into the trough A, and is, after being heated, discharged through the bent-up pipe a', the scum being discharged through a spout, a, lower than the upper part of the discharge-pipe a', but above its connection with the trough, so that none but the clarified juice shall enter the discharge-pipe, and the scum shall rise sufficiently high to be discharged before the juice can escape through the discharge-pipe, to avoid the escape of any impurities with the juice. As the juice circulates through the tubes b it is heated by the waste hot water from the pans, which enters near the top of the vessel B, through a pipe, V, circulates around the tubes, and passes out through a pipe, S, provided with a regulating cock, s. For the purpose of starting the apparatus, and before the sugar-pans are heated, this part of the apparatus is heated by steam from a boiler, which is introduced through a branch pipe, V, which connects with the hot water pipe V. The first modification of this part of the apparatus is represented in same plate, Figs. 4 and 5, and the second modification by Figs. 6 and 7, same plate. The first modification differs only from the above in having the vessel B divided into an upper and lower

compartment by a horizontal diaphragm, and having two pipes, V V, for introducing the hot water to both of them, and two pipes, S S, for discharging it, the hot water for the lower compartment being supplied from the pan working under the lowest pressure to commence heating the juice, and that for the upper compartment from the pan working under higher pressure to increase the heat of the juice as it approaches the top. And the second modification differs from the others in carrying the hot water for heating the juice through two coils of pipes or worms, b', the juice being introduced into the vessel by the same means as above. This apparatus, under either of its forms, can be employed either as a simple heater to heat the saccharine juice to about 175° by the hot water from the pans or boilers, and then to be clarified in the usual way, or, as I prefer it, to clarify the juice by heating it to the boiling point, but without ebullition, as the agitation would prevent the separation of the impurities, which, under the action of heat without ebullition, rise to the top in the form of scum and are discharged at the spout.

From the heater the saccharine juice is conducted to the filters in the usual manner, which does not require to be described or represented, and from these it is discharged in the vat F of the cooler, (see Plate 2,) which is a large flat vessel, and from this it is forced through the pipe N by a force-pump, I, into and through the tubes of a Hall condenser, D'', through which it ascends, and a portion—about one-twentieth—is forced from the top of the condenser through a pipe, o, into the pan B'' of the boiling or evaporating apparatus, and the rest through the pipe z into a vessel, E, which delivers it to a series of horizontal perforated tubes, E'', which discharge it in spray at or near the top of a vertical chamber, G'', down which it falls into the receiving-vat F at the bottom. As the juice descends in the form of spray it is met by a current of air from a rotary fan-blower, G, which cools and partly evaporates it. When thus cooled, it is again forced, as before described, through the tubes of the condenser, and its passage through condenses the vapor from the vacuum-pan B, which escapes from the upper part of the bonnet through a pipe, F', (as represented in Fig. 12 Plate 3,) into the hollow support G', from thence through a valve in the back hollow pillar, V', and thence along a horizontal pipe, W, to the condenser and outside the pipes thereof, (in the well-known manner of the Hall condenser, which needs no representation,) and when condensed the water and air are drawn out by the air-pump H in the usual manner of exhausting a condenser. The vacuum-pan is heated by the vapor from the saccharine juice in the pan B'', and when condensed the hot waste water passes out through the pipe V to the heater; for the purpose before described. The air and feed pump is operated by eccentrics or cranks on the shaft P and the fan-blower G by a belt from the belt-wheel Q on the shaft T, the shafts T and Q being geared together by cog-wheels R, receiving motion from some first mover. As the evaporating apparatus represented in this connection is similar to the one patented by me on the 26th of August, 1843, it is not deemed necessary to give a description of it in this connection, particularly as it must be obvious that my improved methods of heating and clarifying and cooling and condensing can be combined with any kind of evaporating apparatus, and I contemplate employing them in connection with the evaporating apparatus to be hereinafter specified. I have therefore simply described the manner of combining these improvements with an evaporating apparatus for making sugar.

From the foregoing it will be obvious that the effect of this arrangement is to condense the vapor from the vacuum-pans which communicate with the condenser, so that by the circuit the saccharine juice is partly evaporated and prepared for being introduced in the pans while it is used as a means of condensing the vapor from and keeping up a vacuum in the vacuum-pans, thus effecting a leading object of my invention—viz., carrying on the whole operation without the necessity of using water for condensation, as water is frequently very scarce in many of the best sugar-manufacturing regions of the country. The essential features of this part of my invention may, however, be used with water, but without waste, by arranging the apparatus as represented in Plate 3, Figs. 10 and 11. In this modification the quantity of water necessary for carrying on the condensing operation is placed in the vat F, and from this it passes through the pipe N to a common condenser, D″, to form the condensing-jet in the usual manner of working a condenser, and from the condenser it is drawn out and discharged into the hot well k″ by a common single-acting air-pump, H, and from the hot well the water of condensation is forced through the pipe Z by a force-pump, K, or by an air-vessel into the vessel E, which discharges it in spray through the perforated tubes, to be cooled in its descent to the vat F by the current of air from the fan-blower G, as above described. The water evaporated in the cooling-room during the descent of the spray is equal to the water produced in the condenser by the condensation of the vapor from the pans, so that the first charge of water with which the apparatus is started will continue to work it for any length of time.

Of the boiling or evaporating apparatus represented in Figs. 12 and 13 of Plate 3, and Figs. 14, 15, 16, and 17 of Plate 4: The pillars and frame-work that support the pans or boilers are made hollow to answer the purpose of the pipes for conducting liquids to be evaporated, the waste water, and the vapor by which the process is to be carried on.

The evaporating pans or boilers A′ A″ A‴ A⁗ are all constructed alike. They are cylindrical, and the lower half at each end extends beyond the heads to form a chamber, B′ and C′, at each end, the heads being pierced in the lower half to receive the tubes D′, that connect the two chambers. These tubes have a slight inclination downward from the front chamber, B′, to the back one, C′, sufficient to permit the flow of water produced by the condensation of the vapor that passes through them. The top is provided with a bonnet, E′, and within there is a pipe, F′, to take the vapor from the upper part of the bonnet to the front end, through which it passes into the hollow support G′ in front, to be conducted to another pan or boiler. Each pan or boiler is provided with a discharge-pipe, H′, at bottom, governed by a stop-cock, I′, for the purpose of discharging the contents of each boiler when necessary. The series of pans having been properly charged, steam from a boiler or the escape-steam of the engine enters the first hollow pillar, K′, through the pipe L′, passes through the valve M′ into the compartment N′ of the frame-work, which communicates with the front chamber, B′, of the first pan, A′. It circulates through the tubes, heating the saccharine juice in the pan or boiler outside the tubes, and passes off after communicating the required caloric from the back end chamber, C′, through a pipe, O′, which may be in connection with the feed-pump of the steam-boiler, to be pumped back into the steam-boiler, or otherwise used at discretion. The vapor arising from the heated juice in the boiler or pan A′ is drawn off from the upper part of the bonnet E′ by the pipe F′ and conducted to the compartment G′ of the hollow supporting-beam, and passes the valve m′ down the pillar K′ to a receiver, P′. A portion of the vapor from this receiver passes through a pipe, R′, to heat the last or striking pan, A⁗, as will be hereinafter described, and the remnant passes up the hollow pillar K″ through the valve n′, to circulate through the tubes D′ of the boiler A″, to heat and evaporate the more concentrated saccharine juice in the pan A″, which, after being partly evaporated in the first pan, passes to the second through the pipe e, governed by a valve, f. The water produced by the condensation of the steam in passing and heating these tubes in this second pan is carried off in like manner as in the preceding, but may be used for any desired purpose. From this second pan, A″, the vapor is drawn off to heat the third pan, A‴, by a like arrangement of parts as from the first to the second, and the vapor from the saccharine juice in this pan A‴ passes in the same manner as the preceding down the hollow pillar to a receiver, S′, which communicates by the pipes e′ d′ with a condenser, T′, of any desired construction. The sirup from pan A″ passes to the third through the pipe g′, governed by a valve, k′. From the pan A‴ the concentrated sirup passes through the pipe i′ to feed the striking-pan A⁗, which is heated during the operation of the apparatus by a portion of the vapor produced by the evaporation of the saccharine juice in the first pan, A', by means of the pipe R', which connects the hollow pillar K''' with the receiver P'; or it can be heated when the series of sirup-pans are not in operation, or when reboiling molasses by steam from the pipe Q', which branches off from the pillar K' at L', and which may be provided with a valve to shut off this connection when the striking-pan is to be heated by vapor from the first sirup-pan, A'. The vapor from the striking-pan A'''' is drawn off and condensed by connecting the hollow pillar X' and valve l' with the condenser T' by means of the pipe d' and receiver X''', by means of which arrangement the last of the series of sirup-pans, as well as the striking-pan, are connected with the condenser, and this connection can be broken at pleasure by closing either of the valves m'', in the hollow pillar X''' or l' in pillar X''''. The saccharine juice is supplied to the first pan through the pipe o', governed by the valve p', and, after being partly concentrated under the highest degree of temperature, it is drawn into the second pan, A'', to be evaporated *in vacuo* through the pipe e', governed by the valve f', and from this it is transferred to the third pan, A''', to be still further concentrated through the pipe g', governed by the valve h', and from this it is delivered through the pipe i', governed by a valve, j', to the filters, in the usual manner; and from these it is drawn up and transferred to the striking-pan A'''' through the pipe q', governed by a valve, r', to be reduced to the striking or crystallizing point. But if only two sirup-pans should be used instead of three, then the sirup can be drawn off to the filters from the second-pan, A'', through the pipe g' by closing the valve h' and opening the one h'', the third pan and all its connections being closed or dispensed with. Each of the chambers G' connected with the pans is provided with a cleansing and discharging pipe and valve, s'. By this arrangement it will be obvious that when the connection between the hollow pillar K', which conducts steam from a boiler (or the exhaust-steam from an engine) to heat the first pan, A', and the steam-pipe Q', that leads to the striking-pan A'''', the striking-pan will be heated by a portion of the vapor of the saccharine juice in the first pan, A', by means of the connection between the receivers P' and S'', and that therefore the last of the series of sirup-pans, A'', can be connected with the condenser, and that the striking-pan can be worked independent of the sirup-pans in consequence of its connection with the steam-pipe L' or the first or second

of the series of sirup-pans in such manner that either of these connections can be broken at pleasure.

It will be obvious that this boiling or evaporating apparatus can be employed in connection with my improved heater and cooler by adopting the connections pointed out in the description of the entire apparatus.

Having thus pointed out the principle or character of my improvements and the manner of constructing and applying the same, what I claim as my invention, and desire to secure by Letters Patent, is—

1. The method of heating the saccharine juice in a heater preparatory to its introduction in the evaporating-pans, by means of the waste hot water or escape steam from the evaporating-pans, substantially as described.

2. The method of clarifying saccharine juice by heating it in a heater provided with a spout for the discharge of the impurities in the form of scum, and a pipe for drawing off the clear liquid, the said pipe being so arranged as to receive the liquid from the heater below the level of the spout which discharges the scum, and then bending up above the said spout to cause the liquid in the heater to rise sufficiently high to discharge the scum, substantially as described.

3. The method of cooling and partially evaporating saccharine juice or other liquids by discharging the same in the form of spray or drops in a chamber, where it meets with a current of air, substantially as described; and this I also claim in combination with a condenser, substantially as herein described, whereby the liquid intended to be concentrated is prepared for the evaporating-pans and used as a means of condensing the vapor from the pans in which it is to be concentrated, or by means of which the water used for the condensing-jet is recooled, substantially as described.

4. The method, substantially as described, of combining a vacuum striking-pan with a series of evaporating-pans, the last of which is independent of the striking-pan, and the last of the series of evaporating-pans can be in connection with the condenser and work independently of each other, that either the striking-pan or the series of evaporating-pans can be worked without the other, as described.

       N. RILLIEUX.

Witnesses:
 CHS. M. KELLER,
 CH. L. FLEISCHMANN, Jr.

J. Standard
July 14, 1891
#455,891

DAN
HAYES

Frederick McKinley Jones

An orphan at the age of ten, Frederick Jones left school in the sixth grade, in order to fend for himself. He worked as a pin setter, in bowling alleys, and as a water boy, on construction projects. During these early years, he became fascinated by gasoline engines and the intricacies of complicated machinery. By the time he was sixteen, he was competent enough to become a journeyman mechanic, in a Cincinnati garage. At the age of 19, he was shop foreman; and his specialty was building racing cars from the chassis up.

After several years, he moved to Hallock, Minnesota, where he worked at the design and rebuilding of farm equipment. His spare time was spent in building his own racing cars for the dirt track circuit. He broke a number of records, earning the name "Casey" Jones, for his daring driving. During this time, a new field gained his interest, that of electronics. He built a sound track for a local movie house. His techniques were so advanced that he was hired by a manufacturer of movie sound systems.

The next series of events is typical of the circumstances experienced by many of our black inventors, as they pioneered entire new industries — as though such endeavors were "routine job assignments."

Jones' employer had been conducting a running argument with two of his friends, one a trucker and the other a movie-house air conditioning man. The trucker complained bitterly about having truckloads of poultry spoil because the ice had melted. The air conditioning man was frustrated because he could visualize cooling trucks by refrigeration, but did not think the equipment could stand the bouncing around.

Typically, the problem was turned over to the black inventor.

Frederick Jones knew plenty about shock-proofing, from his experience in building racing cars. But, first, he began studying refrigeration at the public library. Then, he collected parts from junk yards and, using a two-cycle engine *(of his own invention and patent), he put together the first practical truck refrigeration system in the world!*

The transportation industry was revolutionized by Jones' invention. The marketing habits of an entire nation were changed as the *inexpensive transportation of frozen foods developed around the concept of a black grammar school drop-out*!

Later the refrigeration systems *for all Army and Marine field kitchens* were designed by Jones. He also designed *the first portable X-ray machine*. And, then, returned to his specialty, when he gave the world one of its most important elements in the field of food economics, *the refrigerated boxcar*!

Frederick M. Jones went on to become the *first black member of the American Society of Refrigeration Engineers* . . . and to give us scores of other patented inventions, which have made our lives more comfortable.

Patent No. 2,163,754	Ticket dispensing machine	June 27, 1939
Patent No. 2,475,841	Air conditioning unit (refrigerated truck)	July 12, 1949
Patent No. 2,696,086	Method for air conditioning (refrigerated boxcar)	December 7, 1954
Patent No. 2,780,923	Method for preserving perishables (refrigerated boxcar)	February 12, 1957
Patent No. 2,532,273	Two-cycle gasoline engine	November 28, 1950
Patent No. 2,376,968	Two-cycle gas engine	May 29, 1945
Patent No. 2,475,842	Starter generator	July 12, 1949
Patent No. 2,417,253	Two-cycle gas engine	March 11, 1947
Patent No. 2,477,377	Means for thermostatically operating gas engines	July 26, 1949
Patent No. 2,504,841	Rotary compressor	April 18, 1950
Patent No. 2,509,099	System for controlling the operation of refrigeration units	May 23,1950

Patent No. 2,526,874	Apparatus for heating or cooling the atmosphere within an enclosure	October 24, 1950
Patent No. 2,535,682	Prefabricated refrigerator construction	December 26, 1950
Patent No. 2,581,956	Refrigeration control device	January 8, 1952
Patent No. 2,666,298	Methods and means of defrosting a cold diffuser	January 19, 1954
Patent No. 2,850,001	Control device for internal combustion engine	September 2, 1958

Fruehauf

Refrigerator Truck

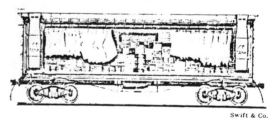

Swift & Co.

Railroad Refrigerator Car

Dec. 7, 1954   F. M. JONES   2,696,086

METHOD AND MEANS FOR AIR CONDITIONING

Filed Jan. 5, 1950   16 Sheets—Sheet 1

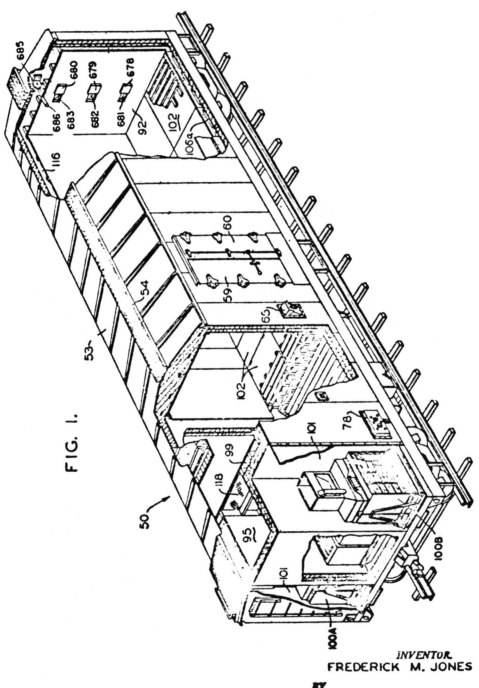

FIG. I.

INVENTOR
FREDERICK M. JONES

BY

Whitely and Caine

ATTORNEYS

Dec. 7, 1954   F. M. JONES   2,696,086

METHOD AND MEANS FOR AIR CONDITIONING

Filed Jan. 5, 1950   16 Sheets—Sheet 2

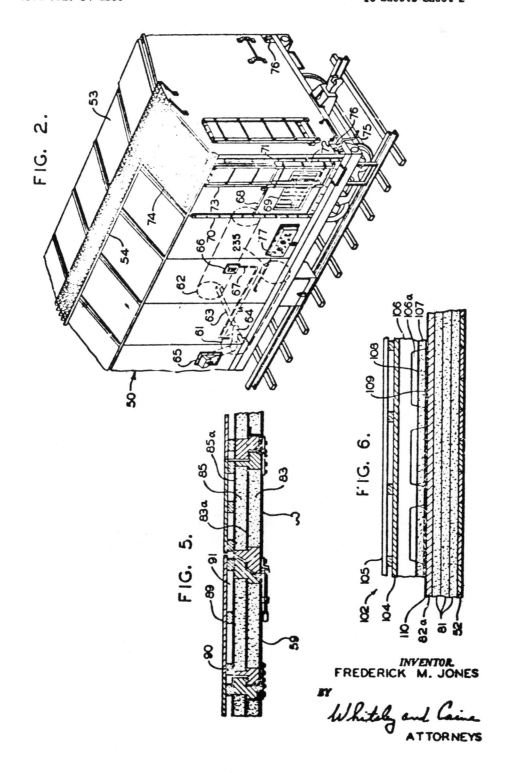

FIG. 2.

FIG. 5.

FIG. 6.

INVENTOR
FREDERICK M. JONES

BY

Whitely and Caine

ATTORNEYS

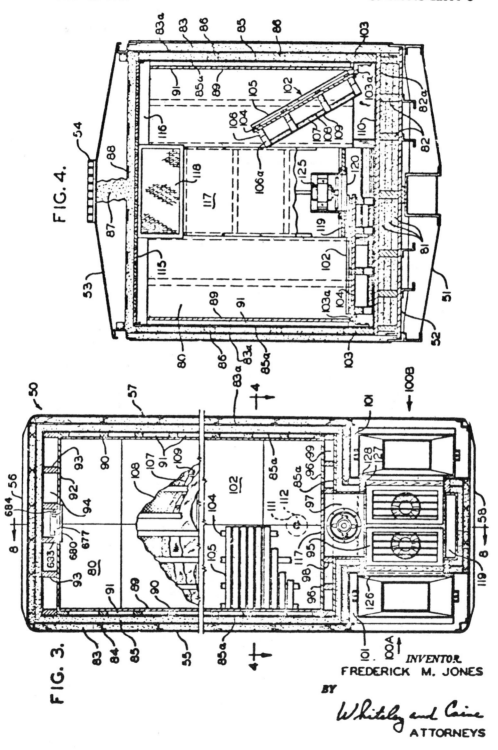

Dec. 7, 1954   F. M. JONES   2,696,086

METHOD AND MEANS FOR AIR CONDITIONING

Filed Jan. 5, 1950   16 Sheets-Sheet 3

FIG. 4.

FIG. 3.

INVENTOR.
FREDERICK M. JONES

BY
Whitely and Caine
ATTORNEYS

Dec. 7, 1954   F. M. JONES   2,696,086

METHOD AND MEANS FOR AIR CONDITIONING

Filed Jan. 5, 1950   16 Sheets-Sheet 4

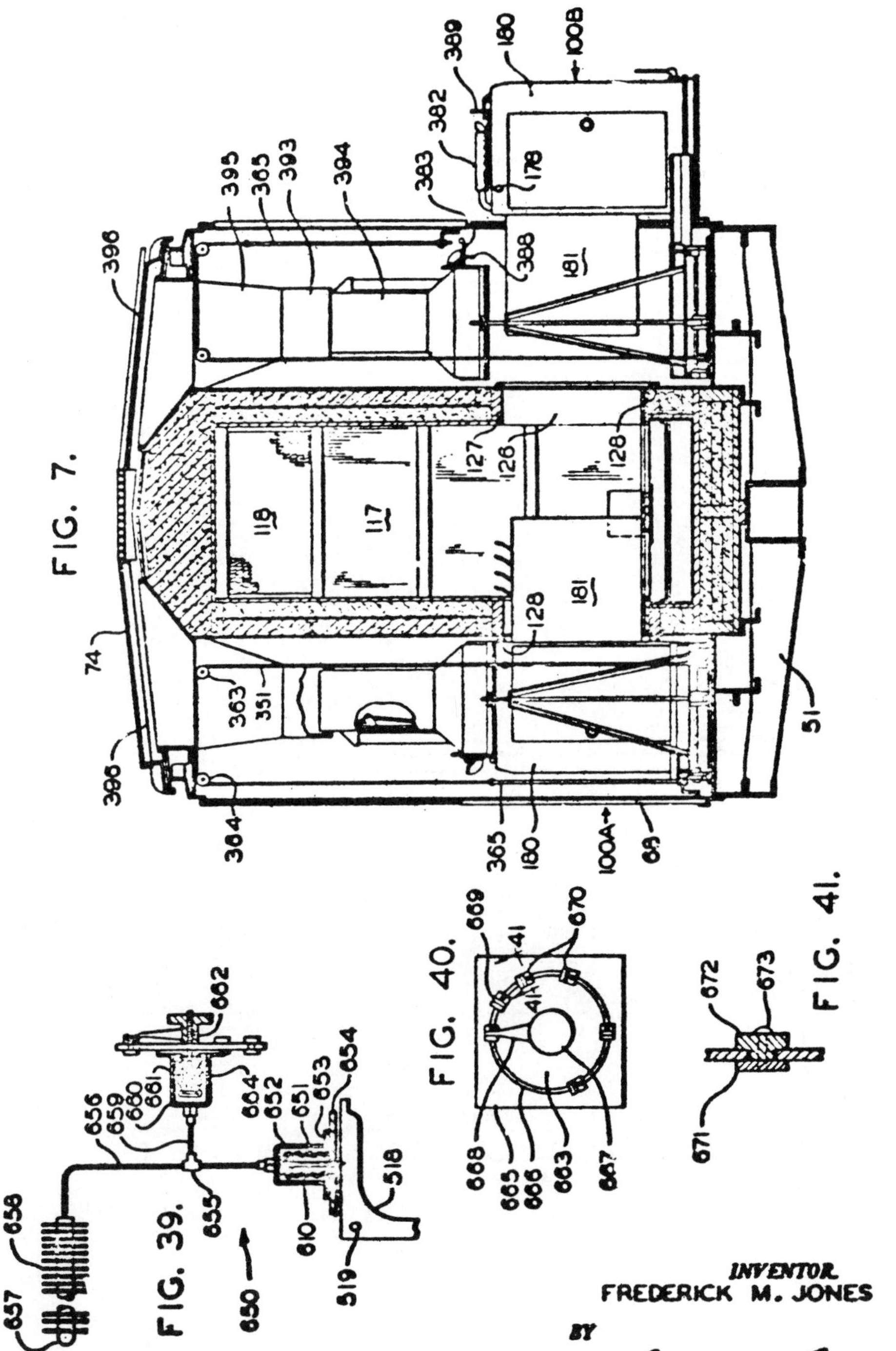

FIG. 7.

FIG. 39.

FIG. 40.

FIG. 41.

INVENTOR
FREDERICK M. JONES

BY

Whitely and Caine

ATTORNEYS

1

2,696,086

METHOD AND MEANS FOR AIR CONDITIONING

Frederick M. Jones, Minneapolis, Minn., assignor to The U. S. Thermo Control Co., Minneapolis, Minn., a corporation of Minnesota

Application January 5, 1950, Serial No. 136,952

32 Claims. (Cl. 62—4)

My invention is related to a method and means of conditioning air and in circulating the same about and through an enclosed storage space. In general, the invention is concerned with a method and means of controlling the temperature and humidity in and about an enclosed space such as the storage space of a transport vehicle used for the transportation of fresh or frozen foodstuffs and the like. More particularly it is concerned with a method and means of providing proper refrigeration within a railway vehicle used for the transportation of fresh or frozen cargoes such as perishable foodstuffs of all varieties and in maintaining substantially constant conditions within the controlled space despite changes in either direction of the atmosphere ambient to the carrier.

In recent years there has been a marked increase in the demand for fresh perishable foodstuffs and it has been a major problem to the transportation industry to transport such products from their source of origin to relatively distant markets because of spoilage in transport. It is estimated that the loss effected by spoilage amounts to approximately one-fourth of the gross value of the product. Moreover, even though complete spoilage may not occur, the task of maintaining the conditions of certain products within an optimum range of temperature during transport is particularly critical, and this is most evident in certain forms of fresh vegetables and frozen foods. As one example, choice grades of eating apples which are maintained under cold storage conditions after harvesting, should be kept at a temperature of substantially 31° F. plus or minus 1°. If the fruit is cooled below 29° F. it will freeze, and if the temperature is permitted to rise for any substantial period of time to a point above 35° F., decomposition sets in and in time the fruit becomes soft and pulpy.

The frozen food industry presents another type of problem. Foods which have been preserved by severe freezing can be kept in practically perfect condition for a year or more if they are maintained at temperatures ranging between —10° F. and 0° F. However, some of these foods such as fish, poultry, orange concentrate, and strawberries, and the like, will either spoil or change in flavor in a matter of hours if their temperature is permitted to rise to as much as +20° F.

Heretofore it has not been possible to maintain a substantially constant temperature within the storage space of refrigerator cars. nor has it been possible to maintain the space within these cars at 0° F. or lower for any substantial period of time.

In the prior art relating to the refrigeration of cargo carriers used on railroads, it has been the general practice to rely on the use of natural ice, or a brine solution refrigerated by ice, as the principal means of cooling the cargo space. In such carriers it is customary to provide bunkers at either ends of the car within which a large amount of ice is placed. Generally by means of fans operated from the wheel mechanism, the atmosphere within the enclosed space is circulated relative to these bunkers to cool the space. This means of providing refrigeration is expensive both from the point of view of the cost of the ice and brine, as well as the destructive effect of the brine upon the cars and associated equipment. In the conventional manner of transporting refrigerated cargoes, it is customary to re-ice the vehicles at stations along the right-of-way which are spaced about 300 to 400 miles apart. This is not only a costly means of refrigeration from the point of view of re-icing, but

2

where there are delays, it frequently happens that the temperature within the cargo space will have substantially exceeded the safe upper limits for the cargo, thus resulting in spoilage for which, if evident, the carrier must pay damages.

In further consideration of the problems arising out of the transportation of perishable products, there are times and occasions when the produce is moved from an area where climatic conditions are relatively warm to or through areas where climatic conditions are relatively cold, and under these conditions it is necessary to prevent the produce from freezing. In the prior art it has been customary to refrigerate the cars as they are passing through the warm climate, and as they approach the area of colder climatic conditions, to remove the ice from the bunkers and provide some means of supplying a small amount of heat to the enclosed space so as to maintain the temperature therein above the freezing point. Quite frequently it occurs that climatic conditions will change, or the cars will be delayed in transit, so that the changeover is delayed and the produce will spoil either by freezing or by such inaccurate control of the temperature as to permit a certain amount of decomposition to set in.

It is proposed to substitute mechanical condition control means to take the place of the natural refrigerating means. I am, of course, aware of the fact that there have been prior attempts made to use mechanical air conditioning means within railway cars. Insofar as I am aware, however, these prior art efforts have not been entirely successful because to a large extent the mechanical apparatus heretofore used has been made a permanent part of the car structure. A principal objection to this arrangement has been that the cost of installing mechanical equipment in the cars is excessive and in order to justify the expense, cars so equipped must be kept in substantially continuous use. Another defect of this arrangement has been that such mechanism, heretofore used, has not been able to withstand vibration and the severe shocks resulting from impact between the locomotive and the cars, and between the cars themselves when a train is being made up or separated. Practically every time a train is made up, the cars are shunted along various tracks where they slam into each other during the connecting operations. Not infrequently cars will be traveling at rates from two to seven or eight miles per hour at the time they impact a string of stationary cars, and the result of such impacts is to cause disconnection of essential parts, and fatigue of other parts which almost always result in leakage of the essential refrigerating fluid. I am further aware of the so-called "package units," one of which is shown and described in Numero and Jones Patent 2,303,857, and another of which is shown in the Jones Reissue Patent 23,000, both of which are assigned to the present assignee. Both of these units are provided with a portion containing the operating mechanism which is normally positioned on the outside of the vehicle, and a condition-changing portion which is normally maintained on the inside of the vehicle. In the one disclosure the unit is mounted beneath the vehicle body while in the other disclosure the unit is mounted in an upper wall portion of the vehicle body. The present invention contemplates certain improvements over either of these former disclosures.

In the present invention I have provided an improved means of controlling both the temperature and the humidity conditions within a transport vehicle by providing what I consider to be an entirely different concept of air conditioning both as to the vehicle, the mechanical apparatus used for controlling the condition of the air, and the control of the mechanical apparatus.

Insofar as the vehicle itself is concerned, I have provided a structure which includes an internal chamber provided with damper controlled vents and which is insulated from the walls of the vehicle and within which the cargo is carried. At one end of the car and within an area which is substantially equal to one of the ice bunkers found in prior art cars, the mechanical air conditioning structure is mounted. The mechanical structure is a complete unit which may be bodily removed from the car, and includes a heat transfer portion which extends into a part of the enclosed chamber but is separated from

3

the cargo-carrying portion by a partition which forms a passage through which the air is passed in heat exchange relationship as it leaves the cargo chamber and is thereafter returned thereto. The separated portion of the chamber actually extends to the one end of a car so as to form separated compartments on either side thereof at the end of the car. Within each of these separated compartments an independent mechanical air conditioning unit is removably mounted through an opening in a lateral side of the car adjacent its end wall. Each of the units is thus carried entirely within the car and has its heat exchange portion extending in opposition to a similar portion of the other unit through restricted openings into the passage located at one end of the chamber.

In one modification the enclosed chamber is composed of five walls of material having a low thermal drop therethrough and is open on its remaining side. In addition to being insulated from the car structure, the chamber is also separated therefrom so as to form an insulated passage or air duct about the five sides of the chamber. This duct or air passage communicates with the heat exchange passage that contains the air conditioning device and a circulating fan. The heat exchange passage communicates with the interior of the cargo chamber adjacent the open side thereof. One of the walls of the cargo chamber is provided with a series of damper controlled openings disposed in spaced relationship across the wall so as to form entry ways between the general air duct and the interior of the chamber and when the dampers are in an open position permit a portion of the circulated air to pass through the interior of the cargo chamber and in direct contact with the lading therein. The damper controlled openings are opened at the outset of the transit period for precooling the cargo space and the cargo itself after loading to assure a quick reduction of the temperature of the cargo to a desired transit temperature, after which the dampers are closed so that the circulated air in the general air passage passes about the exterior of the chamber and in contact with the outer surfaces thereof before returning across the open side thereof to the inlet opening of the heat exchange passage, thus minimizing contact between the circulated air and the lading within the chamber.

Under certain conditions it may be necessary to humidify the air to prevent dehydration of the cargo, and to supply this need, moisture absorbent means is carried by the car over which the conditioned air is passed prior to entering the chamber.

In another modification the conditioned air is introduced directly into the top of the chamber whence it is distributed in proportioned amounts throughout the length of the chamber both at the center and sides thereof to descend into the enclosed space and thereafter be withdrawn at one end of the chamber where, as in the preceding modification, it is passed downwardly over the heat exchange portion before being returned to the chamber.

When the heat exchange portion is operative to change the condition of the air, air circulating means is in continuous operation to continuously move the air cyclically from the chamber downwardly over the heat exchange portion and thence back to the chamber. During periods when the heat exchange portion is inoperative, as by way of a satisfied condition within the chamber, an auxiliary air circulating means is placed in operation, so that the air is always being circulated within the compartment.

In order that the air conditioning units may be readily inserted or removed from the car, they are each mounted on a frame structure which includes a slidably movable portion which is capable of extending outwardly through the opening in the side wall of the car so that the unit may be readily mounted thereon or removed therefrom by a winch. To prevent the units from being tampered with by unauthorized persons, the respective openings through which they are inserted into the car are closed by a sliding door. As these doors occur at the ends of the car, and to provide accommodation for the train crews, each of the doors carries a ladder which telescopically slides with respect to a stationary ladder portion positioned on the car above the door. To prevent the door from being opened by unauthorized persons, a locking mechanism cooperates with the door control means to lock the door in its closed position. To avoid any possibility of a car being dispatched with its doors open, the means for opening and closing the doors constitutes a

4

key for controlling the locking mechanism. This key, which is in the form of a crank, will be supplied only to persons authorized to have access to the air conditioning units.

As the operative portion of each of the air conditioning units includes an internal combustion engine, means must be provided for disposing of the exhaust gases as well as the heat generated by the engines, and for this purpose I have provided within each of the aforementioned compartments a hood structure which includes a vent pipe that extends through the upper wall of the car. The hood structure fits directly over the top of the operating portion of the air conditioning device, but is connected to the frame structure which supports the device so as to be telescopically movable when the door is opened and the device is slidably moved outwardly on its frame for replacement. The hood contains a thermostatically operated damper for returning a portion of the heated air to the operating portion when climatic conditions are such that a portion of the heat should be returned to maintain the engine and its cooperating parts in a heated condition.

The air conditioning units themselves each constitutes a unitary casing within which the several portions of the device are divided into an operating portion including an engine, compressor, condenser, and a fan for cooling the condenser, and a heat transfer portion which includes an evaporator having a driven fan above it for forcing the air downwardly in heat exchange relationship with the evaporator. A set of dampers are mounted in the casing portion above the evaporator and are operable to prevent the circulation of air during a defrosting operation. These dampers, however, will remain open during either heating or cooling of the air. The operation of the dampers is controlled by a fluid system, which is circulated when the engine is operating.

The refrigerant fluid system of the unit, which includes the compressor, condenser and evaporator, are interconnected by a control valve which is operable to completely reverse the flow of refrigerant so that the functions of the evaporator and the condenser may be reversed. The operation of this valve is normally automatic, and is controlled by an electrical system.

As mentioned above, the air conditioning units may be used to either heat or cool the storage chamber, and their operation for either purpose are controlled by a control system which is capable of initially starting and stopping one of the engines in response to the condition within the controlled space. In the event that the one unit is capable of maintaining the desired condition within the controlled space, or should for any reason become inoperative, the control system provides means for initiating the operation of the other unit which normally serves merely as a standby unit. The system also includes means for automatically changing the function of the air conditioning units from cooling units to heating units so as to maintain a substantially constant condition within the controlled space when the vehicle moves through changing climatic conditions. When the units are used in conjunction with a car during the winter season, there is always the possibility that climatic temperatures may be so low as to eventually cause the engines and their cooperating elements, including the lubricating fluid, to be cooled down to an inoperative temperature. This condition could arise when the temperature within the controlled space remains static for a substantial period of time. To remedy these conditions, the control system includes means for starting the engines solely for the purpose of running them long enough so that they will always remain sufficiently heated to be operative.

As has been previously mentioned, during the periods when the air conditioning units are not in operation, one or more fans are provided for circulating the air within the enclosed space to maintain a relatively uniform condition throughout the space. This fan or fans are operated from the battery current normally used for the starting of the engines, each of which has its own set of batteries. Assuming a condition where one of the batteries may be relatively weak from long usage, the electrical system includes means for selecting the source from which the current needed for the fan will be derived.

As a refrigerator car, like any other transport car, is sealed when its cargo is loaded, it is not possible for persons responsible for the safe transport of the cargo to be aware of the conditions within the enclosed space. Ac-

5

cordingly, control panels are mounted on either side of the car adjacent the openings through which the units are inserted. The panels include indicating means for showing the condition of the enclosed storage space and also means for pre-setting the temperature at which the space will be maintained. The panels also include visual means for showing the operating condition of each of the mechanical air conditioning units and is capable of indicating whether these units are operating on either the refrigerating or the heating cycle or if they are momentarily inactive, whether the circuits are in proper condition so that the units are capable of operating when the need requires the same. Since the cars containing these panels will be moved during the hours of daylight and darkness, the last named indicating means include a plurality of lights which will enable an inspector to tell the condition of each of the cars as they are moved past a fixed point.

The supply of fuel necessary for the operation of the engine, and suitable batteries for starting and ignition as well as supplying current for other circuit needs, are carried by the car independent of the units. Means are provided for simply and easily connecting the fuel supply, the current supply and the conductors to and from control portions to the units by easily detachable means so that either unit could be removed in a relatively few minutes and if desired, replaced by another unit.

An object of the invention is to provide an improved method and means of refrigerating or of maintaining in a substantially constant refrigerated condition, perishable foodstuffs and the like so that the same may be stored or transported under the most desirable conditions and without deterioration due to changes in temperature or in moisture content.

Another object is to provide a method of both precooling and refrigerating perishable products in transit by loading the products into an enclosure whose surfaces are composed of material having a low thermal drop therethrough and which surfaces are separated from an insulated wall to form a general air passage in which refrigerated air is circulated, passing some of the circulated air from the passage through the enclosure in one or more short circuit paths for one continuous period until the space or products therein are precooled, thereafter permanently terminating the circulation of the air in the short circuit path through the enclosure and in contact with the product while continuing the circulation of air within the general air passage and in contact with the exterior surfaces of the chamber to maintain the products at reduced temperature principally by thermal transfer through the surfaces of the enclosure.

Another object is to provide a method of both precooling and refrigerating perishable products in transit by loading the products into an enclosure whose surfaces are composed of material having a low thermal drop therethrough and which is open on one side, which enclosure is surrounded by an air duct in which refrigerated air is circulated, passing some of the circulated air through the interior of the enclosure in a short circuit path for one continuous period at the outset of the transit period to reduce the temperature of the space within the enclosure, thereafter permanently terminating the circulation of the air in the short circuit path through the enclosure for the remainder of the transit period while continuing the circulation of the cooled air exterior to the enclosure and across the open side thereof to maintain an envelope of cooled air in contact with the outer surfaces of the enclosure and partially in contact with the atmosphere within the enclosure across the open side thereof to maintain the products at reduced temperature principally by thermal transfer through the surfaces of the enclosure and by some interchange of air across the open side thereof.

Another object is to provide an improved refrigerator vehicle embodying a cargo chamber composed of material having a low thermal drop therethrough and which is open on one side and which is enveloped with an air duct in which refrigerated air may be circulated about the chamber, together with damper controlled openings in one of the chamber walls communicating with the circulated air in the duct.

Another object is to provide a unitary air conditioning unit adapted for use in a railway refrigerator car.

Another object is to provide in combination with a railway car and an air conditioning unit adapted for use therein, means for supporting the unit in such a manner

6

that the same may be readily placed in or removed from the car.

Another object is to provide in combination with a railway car, and an air conditioning unit for use therein, means for supporting the unit in the car in such a manner as to protect the unit from shock and injury resulting from movement and jolting of the car.

Another object is to provide in combination with an air conditioning unit including an internal combustion engine and other parts forming the operating mechanism a protective hood, together with means for recirculating a portion of the heated air from the engine so as to maintain the engine and its associated parts in an operating condition during cold weather.

Another object is to provide an air conditioning unit which is capable of either refrigerating or of heating the space within an enclosure and which is controlled by means which are capable of automatically reversing the heat exchanging function of the unit in response to the condition of the enclosed space.

Another object is to provide in an air conditioning unit which includes an evaporator and a fan for circulating air over the evaporator, a casing surrounding the evaporator having a set of movable dampers between the fan and the evaporator for shutting off the flow of air during a defrosting operation.

Another object is to provide in combination with a mechanical air conditioning unit used to maintain a substantially constant condition within an enclosed space, control means for controlling the operation of the unit in response to a change of temperature within the enclosed space, a condition of the unit itself, or a change of temperature of the air surrounding the enclosed space.

Another object is to provide in combination with a pair of air conditioning units which are not normally under manual supervision, control means for controlling the operation of the units under a plurality of variable conditions which may arise during the absence of manual supervision.

A further object is to provide means for storing or transporting perishable foodstuffs in which the foodstuffs may be refrigerated if necessary, or maintained at a substantially constant temperature and moisture content, which includes a railway car having an internal chamber which is insulated on all sides from the walls of the car and which is supported in spaced relation to several of the walls so as to form an air passage and an area of moisture transfer, together with means for cooling or heating the air to attain or maintain the desired temperature within the internal chamber, and means for automatically controlling the last named means under a variety of varying conditions.

Other and further objects may become apparent from the following specification and claims, and in the appended drawings in which:

Fig. 1 is a perspective view of an improved refrigerator railway car and air conditioning apparatus therefor, with certain parts broken away and others shown in section;

Fig. 2 is a perspective view of a portion of a car seen on a side opposite of that shown in Fig. 1;

Figs. 3–8 are detailed views of the car structure shown in Figs. 1 and 2;

Figs. 9–12 are sectional views of a modified form of refrigerator car;

Figs. 13 and 14 are detailed views of a damper control mechanism used in conjunction with the refrigerator car described in Figs. 9–12;

Figs. 15 and 16 are perspective views of a mechanical air conditioning unit used in conjunction with either of the refrigerator cars disclosed heretofore;

Fig. 17 is a schematic showing of the refrigerant fluid system incorporated in the air conditioning unit disclosed in Fig. 15;

Figs. 18–29 illustrate a structure which supports the air conditioning unit disclosed in Fig. 15 within either of the car structures heretofore disclosed;

Figs. 30A and 30B disclose a portion of a hood structure shown in Fig. 18;

Figs. 31–35 disclose a door operating mechanism and a locking device used in conjunction with either of the cars heretofore disclosed;

Fig. 36 is a schematic diagram of a control system for controlling the operation of a pair of air conditioning units and auxiliary devices used in connection therewith;

Fig. 37 is a schematic diagram on enlarged scale show-

7

ing a portion of the electrical system disclosed in Fig. 36;

Fig. 38 is a schematic diagram of a portion of the control system used in conjunction with the refrigerator car disclosed in Figs. 9–12 and the damper controls shown in Figs. 13 and 14; and,

Figs. 39–41 show a thermostatic control device used in conjunction with the control device schematically shown in Figs. 36 and 37.

Referring now to the several figures of the drawing, the invention will be described in detail. Referring first to Figs. 1–7, general reference numeral 50 designates a railway vehicle ordinarily referred to as a refrigerator car and used for the transportation of perishable foodstuffs and the like. The vehicle includes the conventional undercarriage designated at 51 in Figs. 4 and 7, which is supported on wheels for mobility on railroad tracks, as shown in Figs. 1 and 2. Reference numeral 52 designates a floor surface of the car and reference numeral 53 designates an outer top surface on which is mounted a catwalk 54.

Referring now to Fig. 3, reference numerals 55, 56, 57 and 58 designate the outer lateral walls of the car. Cargo loading doors 59 and 60, Figs. 1 and 5, are mounted on each of the lateral central surfaces of the car for moving the cargo within the interior thereof.

As shown in Fig. 2, supported beneath the undercarriage 51 are a pair of fuel tanks 61 and 62 which are interconnected by a header 63. A conduit 64 extends to a fuel loading opening 65 and a fire-proof breather 66 is secured on the lateral side of the car and connected by a conduit 67 to tank 61 for safety purposes.

On either side of the car, and of which only one is shown in Fig. 2, is a vertically movable door 68 having therein a grill 69. The doors 68 are slidably movable in tracks 70 and 71 on the side of the car. A ladder portion 72 which forms a part of the door structure 68 is telescopically movable with respect to a stationary ladder portion 73 to permit members of a train crew to climb up to a grill 74 located on the top of the car and at one side of the catwalk 54. A crank 75 is provided for controlling the movement of doors 68 and also for locking the same in their closed positions, and this crank is adapted to be removably inserted into socket portions 76 on either side of the end 58 to operate the doors and their respective telescopic ladders.

Also mounted on the outer surface of the car on both sides thereof are a pair of control panels 77 and 78, as seen in Figs. 1 and 2.

Referring now to Figs. 3 and 4, is shown an interior cargo-carrying chamber designated by the general reference numeral 80. The chamber 80, as shown in Figs. 4 and 6, is insulated from the bottom wall 52 by three layers of thermal insulation 81 which are protected by longitudinally extending beams 82 and covered by a wooden floor 82a. The sides of chamber 80 are thermally insulated from the lateral sides of the car by a first layer of thermal insulation 83 which is protected by Z-bars 84 and interior to layer 83 is another layer of thermal insulation 85 which is protected by longitudinally extending beams 86, as shown in Fig. 4. Between the layers 83, 85 is a layer of plywood 83a and on the inner side of layer 85 is a second layer of plywood 85a. The upper surface of the chamber 80 is protected from the top wall 53 by a very thick layer of thermal insulation 87 which is protected by a plurality of longitudinally extending members 88. It should be particularly noted that at all points the thermal insulation is permitted to maintain its original depth or thickness and is at no point compressed, thereby providing a relatively thick thermal wall on all of the interior sides of the car structure.

Referring further to these same figures, the side walls of the chamber 80 are composed of relatively thin sheet members 89 which are spaced from the inner insulating wall surface 85a by a plurality of vertically extending beams 90 so as to form air channels 91 between the outer surface of the wall 89 and the inner surface of the plywood layer 85a. At the end of the chamber 80 adjacent the end wall 56, seen in Fig. 3, panel 92 is separated from the plywood surface 85a by a plurality of beams 93 so as to form a plurality of relatively wide air channels 94.

At its opposite end from that just disclosed, chamber 80 is formed with a bay or compartment 95 which extends through to the end wall 58 and is thermally in-

8

sulated from the outer walls of the car in the same manner as the remainder of the chamber. Panels 96 are positioned on either side of an opening 97 into the inner end of the bay 95 and are spaced from the plywood layer 85a by beams 98 to form air channels 99. On either side of the bay 95 are compartments 101 within each of which is mounted an air conditioning unit indicated by the general reference numerals 100A and 100B and which will be discussed in detail hereinafter.

Referring now to Figs. 1, 3, 4 and 6, the bottom floor of chamber 80 is composed of a plurality of panels designated at 102, each of which is mounted on a side beam 103 by hinges 103a, as shown in Fig. 4, to be elevated when desired. The floor panels 102 are each composed of a layer of wood 104 on which are mounted a plurality of laths 105 to permit air circulation about the cargo. Beneath each of the panels 102 are several longitudinally extending stringers 106 each of which has several cut-out portions 106a, as shown in Fig. 6. Secured to the lower extremities of the stringers 106 and as shown in detail in Fig. 3, is a moisture containing and transferring means in the form of a layer of felt 107 which is covered by a metal screen 108 on its upper surface, and a layer of canvas 109 on its lower surface. As shown in Fig. 8, the moisture absorbing means and particularly the layers of felt 107 which are individually attached to each of the panels 102 are of progressively decreasing thickness as they extend from the end wall 56 towards the end wall 58 of the car. A metal pan 110 having a flat lower surface and upstanding edges is formed as a part of the car underneath the moisture absorbing means and supported on the floor surface 82a, as seen in Fig. 4. The pan itself extends from the end wall 56 to the end wall 58 and is shaped to conform to the structure of the bay 95. As indicated in dotted lines at 111 in Fig. 3, a central plug type drain is provided with a plug 112 for draining and/or washing out the pan 110 when such action is desired.

The top wall of chamber 80, as shown in Fig. 4, consists of a panel 115 which is secured on the lower surface of insulation 87 and extends over the entire top of the chamber. However, it should be noted that the top wall panel 115 is spaced upwardly from the upper extremity of the side walls 89, 92 and 96 so as to form an opening designated at 116 which is in communication with the several air channels 91, 94, and 99 formed on the lateral walls of the chamber.

As shown in Fig. 4, between the end panels 96, and forming a closure for opening 97 is a central panel 117 which completely separates the main chamber 80 from the interior of the bay 95. At its upper extremity panel 117 carries a grill 118.

As seen in Figs. 3, 4, 8, within the interior of bay 95 is a floor surface 119 which is elevated above the surface of panels 102. Floor 119 has a first opening 120, Fig. 4, and in rear of opening 120 are a pair of openings 121 beneath each of the units 100A, 100B, one of which is seen in Fig. 8. As shown in Fig. 8, a plurality of baffles 122 and 123 are mounted on the undersurface of floor 119. At the extreme right, the metal pan 110, mentioned heretofore, terminates in a curved surface designated at 124. Mounted on floor 119 over the opening 120 is an electric fan 125 of more or less conventional construction.

As will be evident in Figs. 7 and 8, the side walls of the bay 95 extend up to the undersurface of the top wall 115 so that bay 95 may, with the exception of the grill 118 be considered as being a passage separated from the chamber 80. As shown in Figs. 3 and 7, each of the side walls of the bay 95 are provided with an enlarged opening 126 which openings are surrounded by a casement 127. On the outer surface of casement 127 is a heavy rubber gasket 128 which is intended to provide a resilient seal with a portion of the air conditioning mechanisms 100 and prevent the entry of outside air into the bay 95.

Referring now to Figs. 9, 10 and 11, is partially shown a modified form of car structure designated by the general reference numeral 130 and from which most of the exterior structure has been eliminated inasmuch as the same is substantially similar to that heretofore described in conjunction with the car structure shown by general reference numeral 50. Reference numeral 131 designates a cargo-containing chamber having a bay portion 132 at one end thereof. Chamber 131 is insulated on all of its several sides by a heavy layer of insulation 133 and on its inner surface is sheathed with plywood at 134 to protect the insulation. Around its side walls and to space the cargo from the plywood 134, are a plurality of spaced laths 135. A plurality of removable floor boards 136 are formed of sections of longitudinally extending stringers 137 which have cross ventilating openings 138 adjacent their lower extremity and support a plurality of transversely extending laths 139 on their upper surface.

As shown in Fig. 11, the side walls of bay 132 form a pair of separated compartments 140, which are identical to the compartments 101 of the car 50. Towards their lower extremity the side walls of the bay are provided with openings 141, each of which is surrounded on its outer edge by a resilient gasket 142. Co-extensive with the lower extremity of the openings 142 is a floorboard 143 which has a pair of openings 144 which are identical to the openings 121 previously described.

As will be evident in Figs. 9 and 11, a pair of metallic ducts 145, 146 extend from each of the openings 142 upwardly in an arcuate manner where they are joined to a single duct member 147. Within the lower portion of each of the ducts 145, 146 are two dividing plates 148, 148a, shown in Fig. 9, and another dividing plate 149 in the central duct 147.

Within the lower portion of each of the ducts 145, 146 are electric heaters 151, 151a for melting ice which may accumulate in the bottom of the ducts. A pair of drain lines 152, 153 extend from each of the ducts through the bottom of the car for draining water which accumulates in the bottom of the ducts as a result of defrosting of the heat exchange coils.

A pair of dampers 154, 155, Fig. 14, are mounted in the ducts 145, 146, and are each separately supported on rods 156, 157 to control the flow of air through the individual ducts to the single duct member 147. Another damper 158 is supported in the single duct 147 on a rod 159 below an opening 160. An electric fan 125 is supported within the opening 160, Fig. 11.

A linkage is provided between the dampers 154, 155 and damper 158 to provide for the closing of damper 158 when either of the dampers 154, 155 are opened, and conversely to open damper 158 only when dampers 154, 155 are both closed. As shown in Figs. 13 and 14, a pair of solenoid operators 162, 163 are supported between the ducts, and as shown in Fig. 13, each of the solenoid operators has a rod 164 connected to a bellcrank lever 165 which supports a roller 166 on its outer end. Above the bellcrank lever 165 is a plate 167 which is solidly mounted on a rod 168 that is surrounded by a coil spring 169. A second plate 170 is supported on rod 168 and is secured to the upper end of the coil spring 169 by a threaded nut 171. The rod 168, as shown in Fig. 13, is angularly bent in opposite angles and at its upper end is pivotally connected at 172 to the damper 158. The solenoid operators 162, 163 are electrically connected in a circuit which will be described hereinafter and which includes means which will energize either of these operators when the respective air conditioning units 100A, 100B are in operation so as to open the dampers 154, 155 when either of these units are started. When the operator is energized, the rod 164 is moved inwardly to cause the bellcrank lever 165 to rotate in a counterclockwise direction bringing the roller 166 in contact with the plate 167 to move the same upwardly, thereby causing rod 168 to move upwardly and close damper 158. When both of the solenoids 162 or 163 are de-energized, the coil spring 169 will cause a return movement of plate 167 so as to move the damper 158 to an open position. A coil spring 173 which is connected to bellcrank lever 165 causes the same to rotate to its inactive position shown in Fig. 13.

Referring now to Fig. 12 in conjunction with Figs. 9, 10 and 11, a partition 174 similar to partition 117 separates the bay 132 from the chamber 131 and this partition supports a large central grill 175 which forms an outlet from the chamber 131 to the bay 132. A tapered duct 176 extends as a continuation of duct 147 through the upper portion of grill 175 into the chamber 131 so as to distribute the air centrally throughout the chamber. A plurality of manually adjustable louvers 177, Fig. 9, provide for the distribution of the air throughout the chamber where it will circulate from the duct 176 down-

wardly throughout the chamber and thence leave the same through grill 175 for return to the bay 132.

Referring now to Figs. 15 and 16, the air conditioning device heretofore referred to by general reference numeral 100, is shown only as to its major elements. The device consists of a general casing 179 which is divided into an operating portion 180 and an air conditioning portion 181 which is of smaller size than portion 180 but forms an integral part of the general casing 179. The two portions are insulatingly divided by a relatively thick wall 182 which is filled with thermal insulation material. Within the operating portion 180 is a prime mover here shown as an internal combustion engine 183 which is directly connected to a starter generator 184 and a multiple grooved drive pulley 185. A compressor, not shown, would normally be supported by a bracket 186 and driven by a shaft 187. On the forward surface of the mechanically operable portion 180 is a refrigerant condenser 188 which is cooled by a blower 189.

The air conditioning portion 181 consists of an evaporator 190, over which air is driven by a vertically positioned blower 191. The upper surface of the portion 181 has a large opening 192 within which are mounted a plurality of dampers 193 connected to a rod 194 whose movement is controlled by means disclosed in Fig. 16.

The blower 189 is operated by a belt 195 which extends around the pulley 185 and thence around a pair of idler pulleys 196, 197 before it connects with a pulley 198 that forms a part of the blower 189. A second belt 199 extends from the pulley 185 around idler pulleys 200, 201 and thence around a pulley 202 which is enclosed within a box-like structure 203 above the blower 191. The belt 199 extends through a relatively narrow passage 204 that penetrates the wall 182 so that the atmosphere within the mechanically operated portion 180 will only be permitted to pass into the box-like structure 203 and not into the general opening 192 on the upper side of the evaporator. It will also be noted that by virtue of the idler pulleys 200, 201, which are adjustably supported in brackets 207 and 208 that the blower 191 is operated at an angle with respect to the driven pulley 185.

Referring now to Fig. 16, is shown the means for operating the dampers 193. Indicated at 210 is an oil reservoir which has a conventional dip stick liquid level indicator 211. The tank 210 is connected by an inlet conduit 212 to the crankcase of engine 183. A second conduit 213 forms a return conduit from the oil pumping system within the engine to tank 210. A third conduit 214 extends from a portion of the lubricating system to a T 215. While not shown, T 215 has a small internal orifice connection with conduit 214 which is in the neighborhood of 1/16 of an inch in diameter. One side of T 215 is connected by a conduit 216 to piston chamber 217 which contains a piston, not shown, having at its upper end a rod 218. A conduit 219 extends from the piston chamber 217 to a T 220 that is in turn connected to a conduit 221 which forms a return line to the oil tank 210. A breather pipe 222 is connected to tank 210 adjacent conduit 221. Between the T's 215 and 220 are conduits 223 and 224 and interconnected between the inner ends of these conduits is a solenoid valve 225. It might here be mentioned that the fluid passage through valve 225 is about 3/16 of an inch in diameter and is substantially greater than the orifice opening from conduit 214.

At its upper end the piston rod 218 is connected to a lever 226 which forms a part of a bell crank lever 227. Extending from the bellcrank lever 227 is a rod 228 that is joined to one end of the damper operating lever 194. A coil spring 229 is connected between lever 194 and a part of the heat exchange casing 181. Also connected to bellcrank lever 227 is a rod 230 which at its lower end is joined to a bellcrank lever 231 that is in turn connected to a rod 232 which has a visual indicator 233 on its outer end that projects through an opening 234 in the operating portion 180 of the general casing 179.

Briefly, the operation of the dampers is as follows: Normally the dampers are closed and will remain in that position under the influence of spring 229. When the engine 183 is in operation, oil from its lubricating system will be under pressure and a portion of this oil will travel through conduit 214 into the T 215 and thence through the conduit 216 to the piston chamber

2,696,086

37

temperature by thermal transfer through the surfaces of the enclosure.

30. A method of precooling and refrigerating perishable products in transit, comprising loading the products within an enclosure composed of material having a low thermal drop therethrough, and which is open on one side, forming a confined body of air which is isolated from ambient atmosphere and which envelopes the enclosure including the open side thereof, forcibly circulating the confined body of air in heat exchange relationship with a refrigerant exterior to the enclosure to effect cooling of the confined body of air, continuously passing a portion of the confined body of air through the interior of the enclosure for one period of time during transit of the product to reduce the temperature thereof, and thereafter permanently terminating the passage of cooled air through the enclosure for the remainder of the transit period while continuing the circulation of the cooled air exterior to the enclosure and across the open side thereof when the temperature of the circulated air is above a predetermined minimum temperature to maintain an envelope of cooled air within the confined space in contact with the outer surfaces of the enclosure and partially in contact with the atmosphere within the enclosure to maintain the products at reduced temperature by thermal transfer through the surfaces of the enclosure and by interchange of air across the open side thereof.

31. A method of preserving fresh perishable food products in transit, comprising loading the products in an enclosure whose surfaces are composed of material having a low thermal drop therethrough, forming a confined body of air that envelopes the enclosure and is substantially isolated from heat exchange with ambient atmosphere, forcibly circulating the confined body of air in heat exchange relationship with a refrigerant heat exchanger exterior to the enclosure to reduce the temperature thereof and cool the enclosure, passing a portion of the circulated air in short circuit paths through the interior of the enclosure in contact with the products and thence in contact with the refrigerant heat exchanger for one continuous period during initial stages of transit to refrigerate the products and transfer moisture from the interior of the enclosure to the heat exchanger and prevent its subsequent deposition within the interior of the enclosure, and thereafter permanently terminating the short circuiting of the circulated air through the interior of the enclosure for the remainder of the transit period to minimize contact between the products and the circulated air, while continuing the circulation of the confined body of air that envelopes the enclosure in heat exchange relationship with the heat exchanger when the temperature of the circulated air is above a predetermined minimum temperature to maintain the products at reduced temperature by thermal transfer through the surfaces of the enclosure.

32. A method of preserving frozen food products in transit, comprising loading the products in a precooled enclosure whose surfaces are composed of material having a low thermal drop therethrough, forming a confined body of air that envelopes the enclosure and is substantially isolated from heat exchange with ambient atmosphere, forcibly circulating the confined body of air in heat exchange relationship with a refrigerant heat exchanger exterior to the enclosure to reduce the temperature of the circulated air to at least the temperature of the frozen foods and concurrently reduce the moisture content of the air, passing a portion of the refrigerated

38

circulated air in short circuit paths through the interior of the enclosure in contact with the products and thence in contact with the refrigerant heat exchanger for one continuous period during initial stages of transit to transfer moisture from the interior of the enclosure to the heat exchanger and prevent its subsequent deposition within the interior of the enclosure, and thereafter permanently terminating the short circuiting of the circulated air through the interior of the enclosure for the remainder of the transit period to minimize contact between the products and the circulated air, while continuing the circulation of the confined body of air exterior to the enclosure in heat exchange relationship with the refrigerant heat exchanger when the temperature of the circulated air is above a predetermined minimum temperature to provide an envelope of refrigerated air about the enclosure and maintain the frozen foods at reduced temperature by thermal transfer through the surfaces of the enclosure.

References Cited in the file of this patent

UNITED STATES PATENTS

Number	Name	Date
Re. 23,000	Jones	May 11, 1948
612,486	Crocker, Jr.	Oct. 18, 1898
668,033	Bohm	Feb. 12, 1901
1,264,899	Clark	May 7, 1918
1,414,669	Reichold	May 2, 1922
1,703,318	Muffly	Feb. 26, 1929
1,789,916	Thornton	Jan. 20, 1931
1,825,694	Hobart	Oct. 6, 1931
1,837,786	Mather	Dec. 22, 1931
1,855,989	Rowledge	Apr. 26, 1932
1,986,863	Terry	Jan. 8, 1935
2,053,974	Smith	Sept. 8, 1936
2,068,435	Rutishauser	Jan. 19, 1937
2,092,085	Riley	Sept. 7, 1937
2,092,981	Lundvall	Sept. 14, 1937
2,102,354	Chambers	Dec. 14, 1937
2,130,089	Hull	Sept. 13, 1938
2,152,291	Starr et al.	Mar. 28, 1939
2,153,297	Butler	Apr. 4, 1939
2,180,974	Atchison et al.	Nov. 21, 1939
2,256,182	Winship	Sept. 16, 1941
2,263,476	Sunday	Nov. 18, 1941
2,303,857	Numero et al.	Dec. 1, 1942
2,351,140	McCloy	June 13, 1944
2,382,084	Mathews	Aug. 14, 1945
2,437,417	Bookman	Mar. 9, 1948
2,453,095	McGrath	Nov. 2, 1948
2,462,514	Lehane et al.	Feb. 22, 1949
2,463,027	Free	Mar. 1, 1949
2,475,841	Jones	July 12, 1949
2,479,128	Maniscalco	Aug. 16, 1949
2,502,893	Schmidt et al.	Apr. 4, 1950
2,511,877	Protzeller	June 20, 1950
2,513,373	Sporn et al.	July 4, 1950
2,523,749	Wilson	Sept. 26, 1950
2,571,445	Hawkes	Oct. 16, 1951
2,585,748	De Silvestro	Feb. 12, 1952
2,612,026	Hansen et al.	Sept. 30, 1952

FOREIGN PATENTS

Number	Country	Date
376,821	Great Britain	July 18, 1932

Elijah J. McCoy

Elijah J. McCoy, the son of runaway slaves, was born in Canada. His father, by dint of hard labor in the Northwest woods, managed to send a teenaged McCoy to Scotland, for an education in mechanical engineering. Upon return to the United States, the already-imaginative young engineer settled in Ypsilanti, Michigan.

In 1870, he began experimenting with lubricators for steam engines. At this period, one of the biggest problems in American industry was "down-time"; this was due to the fact that machinery (and production) had to be halted, while lubrication was performed by hand oilers. Engineering-economists, in analyses of the American economy for the post-Civil War period, have estimated such losses to have been a full 22 percent of the Gross Product or service. McCoy's driving ambition was to find some method whereby machines could be oiled as they worked.

In 1872, working in his own tiny machine shop, he developed a container, or cup, with a tiny stop-cock . . . that regulated the flow of oil onto moving elements of machines. This was the first automatic lubricator and since this date (July 23, 1872, Patent No. 129,843), *millions of machines all over the world have been equipped with some version of his invention . . . including the moon-exploration vehicles.*

Whether is was a matter of Naval vessels, oil-drilling rigs, locomotives, saw mill equipment, mining or construction machinery . . . no one would even consider a purchase . . . unless inspection revealed that it was equipped with the "Real McCoy." That is how a black man's name became a by-word in the industrial sectors of the world.

McCoy went to patent over 50 lubricating units and 25 other ingenious mechanical devices useful not only to industry — but to all mankind. For example, the lawn sprinkler (Patent No. 631,549, September 26, 1899).

Think of the millions of machines since 1872 that have been dependent on McCoy's lubricating units, and of the millions of new machines — in the future — that will be equally dependent on this black man's inventions.

E. McCOY.

Improvement in Lubricators for Steam-Engines.

No. 130,305.   Patented Aug. 6, 1872.

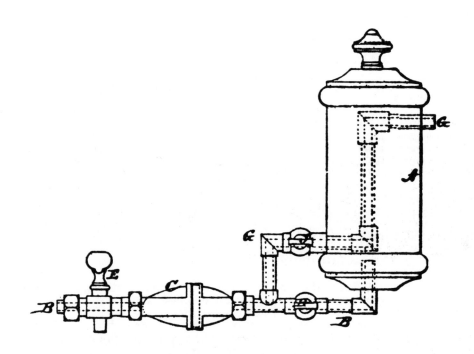

Witnesses: Inventor.
Jas E Calchmore   Elijah McCoy,
C. L. Ewert.   per Frank Thuon
                                              Attorneys.

UNITED STATES PATENT OFFICE.

ELIJAH McCOY, OF YPSILANTI, MICHIGAN.

IMPROVEMENT IN LUBRICATORS FOR STEAM-ENGINES.

Specification forming part of Letters Patent No. **130,305**, dated August 6, 1872.

To all whom it may concern:

Be it known that I, ELIJAH McCoy, of Ypsilanti, in the county of Washtenaw and in the State of Michigan, have invented certain new and useful Improvements in a Lubricator for Cylinders; and do hereby declare that the following is a full, clear, and exact description thereof, reference being had to the accompanying drawing and to the letters of reference marked thereon, making a part of this specification.

The nature of my invention consists in the construction and arrangement of a "steam-cylinder lubricator," as will be hereinafter more fully set forth.

In order to enable others skilled in the art to which my invention appertains to make and use the same, I will now proceed to describe its construction and operation, referring to the annexed drawing, which represents a side elevation of my invention.

A represents the vessel in which the oil is contained, and from the bottom of which a pipe, B, leads to the steam-chest. This pipe is, at a suitable point, provided with a globe or reservoir, C. Between the vessel A and the globe or reservoir C is a stop-cock, D, in the pipe B, and in the same pipe, between the globe and the steam-chest, is another stop-cock, E. A steam-pipe, G, passes from the dome or boiler down through the vessel and connects with the oil-pipe B at the glove or reservoir C, or at any point between the same

and the valve D. In the steam-pipe G, after it leaves the vessel A, is a stop-cock, J. One of these oilers is to be placed on each side of the smoke-arch directly opposite the cylinders, and the various stop-cocks should be so connected with levers or rods that they can be operated simultaneously by a single rod in the engineer's cab. When the engine is working the stop-cocks E and J are closed and the stop-cock D opened, allowing the oil to pass into the globe or reservoir C. The steam being in the pipe G prevents the oil from congealing in cold weather in the vessel A. When the cylinder is to be oiled the stop-cocks E and J are opened and D closed. Steam passing from the boiler or dome through the pipe G forces the oil out of the globe or reservoir C into the cylinder.

Having thus fully described my invention, what I claim as new, and desire to secure by Letters Patent, is—

The combination of the vessel A, oil-pipe B with reservoir C and stop-cocks D E, and the steam-pipe G with the stop-cock J, all constructed and arranged substantially as and for the purposes herein set forth.

In testimony that I claim the foregoing I have hereunto set my hand this 28th day of June, 1872.

ELIJAH McCOY.

Witnesses:
E. P. ALLEN,
ALBERT GROVE.

110

(No Model.)

E. McCOY.

LUBRICATOR.

No. 261,166.

Patented July 18, 1882.

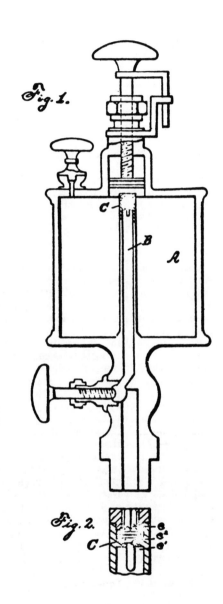

WITNESSES

Samuel E. Thomas

J. Edward Warren

INVENTOR

Elijah McCoy

By W. W. Leggett

Attorney

111

UNITED STATES PATENT OFFICE.

ELIJAH McCOY, OF DETROIT, MICHIGAN, ASSIGNOR TO HENRY C. HODGES
AND CHARLES C. HODGES.

LUBRICATOR.

SPECIFICATION forming part of Letters Patent No. 261,166, dated July 18, 1882.

Application filed June 6, 1882. (No model.)

To all whom it may concern:

Be it known that I, ELIJAH McCOY, of Detroit city, county of Wayne, State of Michigan, have invented a new and useful Improvement in Lubricators; and I declare the following to be a full, clear, and exact description of the same, such as will enable others skilled in the art to which it pertains to make and use it, reference being had to the accompanying drawings, which form a part of this specification.

My invention consists in the combinations of devices and appliances hereinafter specified, and more particularly pointed out in the claims.

In the drawings, Figure 1 represents in outline a lubricator embodying my invention. Fig. 2 is an enlarged view of the valve mechanism at the top of the oil-exit pipe.

This invention is designed more particularly for use upon locomotive-engines, and in other similar locations.

In the running of a locomotive-engine it is customary, when nearing a station or going down a grade, to shut off the steam from the cylinders, and at such times the "cylinder," as it is termed, works a vacuum.

In ordinary use a steam-engine lubricator has the pressure of steam within it, and it is made to operate under those conditions. In case of a locomotive-engine, however, when it works a vacuum, as above explained, whatever oil there is in the lubricator above the discharge-orifice is instantly sucked out into the cylinder and wasted, and this frequently will operate to empty the cup of its oil.

It is the object of this invention to overcome this difficulty. This can be accomplished by a valve in the oil-exit pipe, which will close tight whenever the piston is working without steam; but it is desirable that at that time enough oil may continue to feed to the cylinder to lubricate it while so operating. So, again, when steam enters the lubricator from the cylinder it is apt to suddenly drive out from the lubricator a quantity of oil, and it is desirable that this should likewise be prevented.

In carrying out my invention, A represents any ordinary steam-cylinder lubricator. B is its discharge-pipe, through which oil flows to the parts to be lubricated. C is a valve located in said discharge-pipe, and preferably at its upper end. This valve is made to seat in both directions, up and down. Its upper seat, however, is serrated in any suitable manner, as shown at c, so that the valve cannot seat closely, but will permit quite a free passage past the valve after it has seated at this point. The lower part of the valve seats at c'. This seat is made close, but the valve is provided with a small groove, c².

The operation of the device is substantially as follows: When steam from the cylinder reacts within the lubricator so as to disturb the equilibrium of its contents it will lift this valve C and momentarily hold it up against the upper seat. By so doing the free passage of oil is materially impeded, and any tendency of too great escape at this moment is thereby neutralized, while a sufficient amount is permitted to pass through the serrations c past the valve. Now, when steam is shut off from the cylinder the vacuum produced causes the valve C to close down upon the seat c' below. This prevents the oil from being sucked out from the cup; but the small groove c² affords an outlet for a sufficient quantity of the oil to lubricate the cylinder when its piston is operating without steam. The valve, being a free check-valve, will wear the seats uniformly, and the groove c² on the bottom of the valve is at each operation of the valve opened freely, so that oil constantly scours and keeps the passage free and clear. I have found in practice that by far the best results are obtained by locating this valve at the extreme upper end of the oil-exit pipe, in which position the valve is not materially impeded in its operation by a liquid column, such as would exist if it were located lower down in the exit-pipe.

A lubricator made with this valve mechanism will lubricate an engine through a much longer travel and with much less oil than if the valve be omitted.

Instead of grooving the face of the lower valve, its seat may be grooved, though I prefer to make the groove in the face of the valve. The serrations c being immediately adjacent to the valve, it follows that in the ordinary operations of the cup no column of oil rests upon

2   **261,166**

the valve, but the column is wasted from its base.

What I claim is—

1. The combination, with a lubricator, of a double valve in its oil-exit conduit, said valve provided with an upper serrated seat, and the valve itself grooved in its lower face or seat, substantially as and for the purpose described.

2. The combination, with a lubricator, of an oil-exit pipe provided with a double valve at its upper extremity, said valve provided with an upper serrated seat and with a groove on the lower face of the valve or its seat, substantially as and for the purpose described.

In testimony whereof I sign this specification in the presence of two witnesses.

ELIJAH McCOY.

Witnesses:
J. EDWARD WARREN,
SAMUEL E. THOMAS.

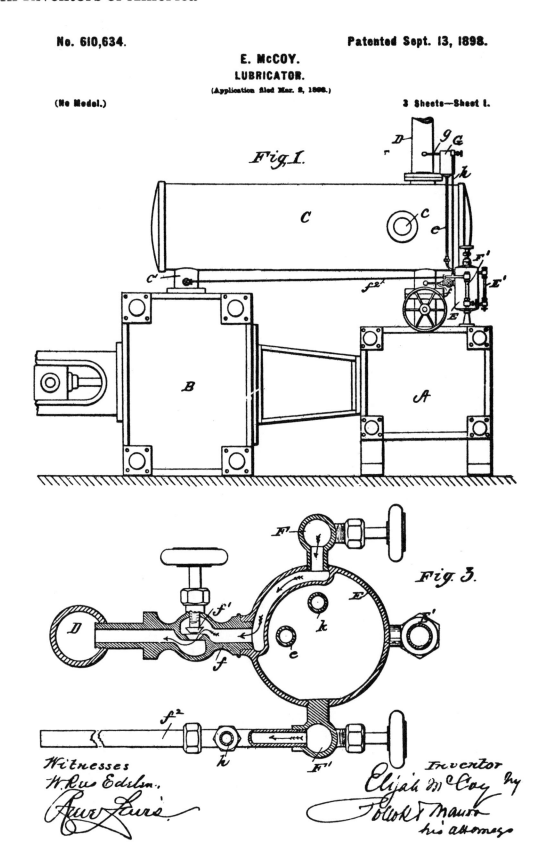

No. 610,634.

Patented Sept. 13, 1898.

E. McCOY.

LUBRICATOR.

(Application filed Mar. 2, 1898.)

(No Model.)

3 Sheets—Sheet 1.

Fig. 1.

Fig. 3.

Witnesses

W. Rus Edelin.

Inventor

Elijah McCoy

his attorneys

No. 610,634.

E. McCOY.
LUBRICATOR.
(Application filed Mar. 2, 1898.)

Patented Sept. 13, 1898.

(No Model.)

3 Sheets—Sheet 2.

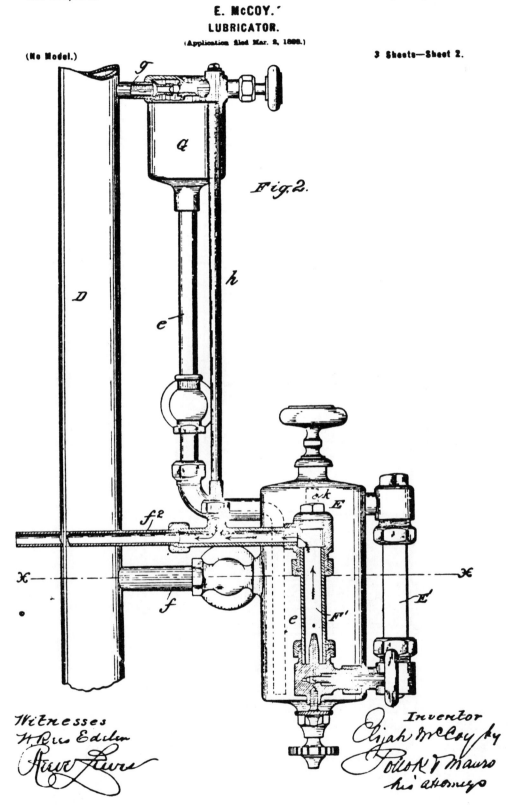

Fig.2.

Witnesses

Inventor

Elijah McCoy by
Polok & Mauro
his attorneys

No. 610,634.

E. McCOY.
LUBRICATOR.
(Application filed Mar. 2, 1898.)

Patented Sept. 13, 1898.

(No Model.)

3 Sheets—Sheet 3.

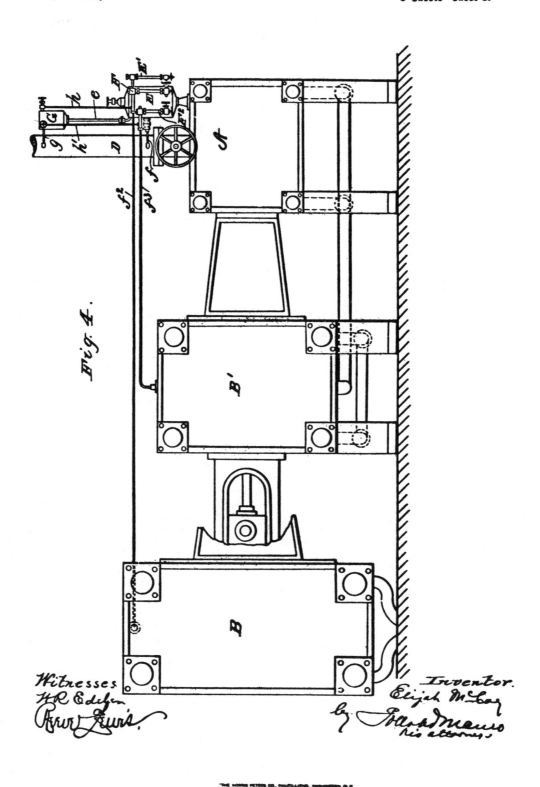

Fig. 4.

Witnesses

Inventor.
Elijah McCoy
by his attorneys,

UNITED STATES PATENT OFFICE.

ELIJAH McCOY, OF DETROIT, MICHIGAN, ASSIGNOR TO THE DETROIT SHEET
METAL AND BRASS WORKS, OF SAME PLACE.

LUBRICATOR.

SPECIFICATION forming part of Letters Patent No. 610,634, dated September 13, 1898.

Application filed March 2, 1898. Serial No. 672,277. (No model.)

To all whom it may concern:

Be it known that I, ELIJAH McCoy, of Detroit, Michigan, have invented a new and useful Improvement in Lubricators, which
5 improvement is fully set forth in the following specification.

My present invention has reference to lubricators, and particularly to lubricators operating upon the principle of condensation
10 displacement for feeding oil to the several cylinders of a multiple-expansion steam-engine through pipes leading thereto. In such lubricators it is necessary to provide means for propelling the oil through the pipe or pipes
15 leading into the intermediate or low pressure cylinder or cylinders, into which pipe or pipes the oil passes from the sight-feeds. Such means is, however, not necessary in connection with the pipe or passage from the
20 sight-feed for the high-pressure cylinder into the main steam-pipe, as the suction created by the passage of steam through the latter is sufficient to draw the oil through said pipe or passage into the main steam-pipe, whereby
25 it passes into the high-pressure cylinder.

With the above-indicated object in view it has been customary to utilize a jet of steam taken from the main steam-pipe through a tube or passage which branches to the sev-
30 eral pipes for conveying oil to the respective cylinders. In practical use, however, it has been found that this arrangement does not operate, as intended, to feed oil in proper proportion (regulated by the valves at the
35 lower ends of the sight-feeds) to the several cylinders, but that a very serious difficulty and defect exists in that the lubricant instead of passing in said proper proportion to the respective cylinders practically all passes to
40 the low-pressure cylinder, leaving the high and intermediate pressure cylinders unlubricated and necessitating the use of ordinary hand-pumps for supplying the requisite quantity of lubricant to the latter or entailing
45 the expense of a separate sight-feed lubricator for each cylinder. This heretofore-unexplained defect in the operation of such devices I have found to be due to the fact that the steam passing through the tube which
50 communicates with the main steam-pipe in-

stead of dividing into the branches leading to the high and intermediate pressure cylinders (in the case of a triple-expansion engine, for example) will all pass through the
55 pipe leading to the low-pressure cylinder, as this pipe offers the path of least resistance. The result is that the oil in the pipes extending to the high and intermediate pressure cylinders is all drawn into the pipe leading to
60 the low-pressure cylinder. The object of my present invention is to overcome this defect and to provide means whereby the proper quantity of oil will be fed to each cylinder irrespective of the difference in pressure be-
65 tween the several cylinders. This is accomplished by providing independent steam-supply passages for the pipes conveying oil from the sight-feeds of the low and intermediate pressure cylinders, communicating with the
70 main steam-pipe at any suitable point or points a sufficient distance above the entrance thereto of the passage conducting oil for the high-pressure cylinder so that such oil in atomized form could not possibly be drawn
75 upwardly in the main steam-pipe and pass into the auxiliary steam-pipe and thence to the low-pressure cylinder. By the arrangement above indicated it will be observed that branches from a common auxiliary steam-
80 pipe to the pipes leading, respectively, to the low and intermediate pressure cylinders are avoided, and hence such defective operation as hereinbefore described is rendered impossible.

85 I have found it convenient and advantageous in practice to arrange the independent auxiliary steam pipe or pipes vertically, connecting them at their lower ends to the oil-supply pipe or pipes, respectively, for con-
90 ducting the oil from the top of the sight-feed or sight-feeds to the intermediate or low pressure cylinders and at their upper ends leading them into the upper end of the condensing-chamber, the latter being arranged
95 at the upper extremity of the hydrostatic column, as herein shown, (and as more fully described and claimed in my application filed December 4, 1896, Serial No. 614,443,) from which the water is fed to displace the oil in
100 the reservoir; but any other suitable arrange-

117

ment may be employed. For example, the independent auxiliary steam-pipes may each be separately tapped into the main steam-pipe at suitable elevation above the inlet to the latter for the oil which passes to the high-pressure cylinder.

My invention will be more fully understood by reference to the accompanying drawings, wherein—

Figure 1 is a side elevation of a horizontal compound engine having my invention applied thereto. Fig. 2 is an enlarged side elevation of the lubricator and main steam-pipe, parts being in section. Fig. 3 is a horizontal section on line $x\,x$, Fig. 2; and Fig. 4 is a view similar to Fig. 1 of a triple-expansion engine.

Referring to Figs. 1 to 3 of the drawings, A represents the high-pressure cylinder, and B the low-pressure cylinder.

C is the steam-chamber, into which steam passes by an opening c from the high-pressure cylinder through a pipe. (Not shown.) D is the main steam-pipe from the boiler, passing downwardly through said steam-chamber, where it acts as a superheater for steam passing through the latter into the high-pressure cylinder.

c' is the steam-exit from the chamber C into the low-pressure cylinder.

E is the oil-reservoir of a double-connection condensation - displacement lubricator, which may be of any suitable well-known construction, provided with a gage-glass E' and sight-feeds F F' for the high and low pressure cylinders, respectively, said sight-feeds connecting with oil-exit pipe k in the reservoir.

e is the condenser-tube, leading into the oil-reservoir from the bottom of the condenser G, located at the upper end of said tube and communicating with the main steam-pipe through a support-arm g.

The parts of the apparatus as thus far described may be of any suitable well-known construction and constitute no part of my present invention.

From the upper end of the sight-feed F the oil fed through the latter is conveyed through support-arm f to the main steam-pipe, down which it is carried to the high-pressure cylinder, the passage through pipe f being controlled by a valve f'. f^2 is another pipe by which oil fed through the sight-feed F' is conveyed to the low-pressure cylinder through passage c', into which said pipe f^2 leads.

h is an independent auxiliary steam-pipe leading into pipe f^2 at its lower end at a point near the sight-feed and at its upper end connected into the upper part of condenser G above the level of support-arm g, so that any overflow of water of condensation will pass through said arm and down the main steam-pipe and not down pipe h.

An important advantage gained by tapping the auxiliary steam-pipes h into the upper part of the condensing-chamber is that the latter affords an area of surface which will readily accommodate a large number of such pipes when the lubricator is used in connection with engines having many expansion-cylinders, at the same time dispensing with many joints and connections which would be necessary in case such auxiliary pipes were separately tapped into the main steam-pipe or into the pipe leading into the top of the condenser from said main steam-pipe. It also affords a construction which can be readily applied to lubricators of this general character now in use by a mere substitution of parts and at comparatively slight expense.

The operation of my improved lubricator is as follows: The water admitted beneath the oil from the hydrostatic column formed in the condenser-pipe e and condenser G displaces oil in the reservoir E, causing the same to be fed in drops upwardly through the sight-feed glasses F F' (the rapidity of such feed being controlled by adjustment of the valves admitting oil to the sight-feeds) and into the pipes f and f^2, where it immediately becomes atomized or vaporized by the steam in said pipes. From the support-arm f the vaporized oil is drawn into the main steam-pipe by reason of a slight suction due to the passage of steam therethrough into the high-pressure cylinder. In the pipe f^2 the vaporized oil is propelled along to the low-pressure cylinder by the jet of steam passing into and through said pipe from independent steam-pipe h. There being no possible way in which the vaporized oil in the pipe f could pass into the pipe f^2 and to the low-pressure cylinder, the high-pressure cylinder receives its proper proportion of the lubricant.

When applied to triple-expansion engines, as shown in Fig. 4, a second independent steam-pipe h' will connect from the upper part of the condenser G into the oil-feed pipe f^3, leading from the sight-feed F² (corresponding to the intermediate cylinder) to the intermediate-pressure cylinder B', the possibility of all the oil feeding to the low-pressure cylinder (as occurs in the lubricators of this type now ordinarily employed) being avoided by the arrangement of the auxiliary steam-pipes above described.

Among the features of construction which are particularly to be observed are, first, that the hydrostatic column is not tapped, as in many old constructions, and which diminishes the effectiveness of the column, and, second, that the low and high or intermediate pressure oil-supply pipes do not go through the same support-arm, as in old constructions, the effect of which is, as already pointed out, to establish a communication between these two pipes, with the result that all or far the greater part of the lubricant goes to the low-pressure cylinder.

While for purpose of economy and convenience of construction it is desirable to connect the independent auxiliary steam-pipe (or pipes) at its upper end to the condensing-chamber, said pipe could with equally as good operative results be tapped into the main steam-pipe at any convenient point above the pipe f. Such and many other deviations from the precise construction illustrated and described will be understood to be fully within the scope and principle of my invention.

Having thus described my invention, what I claim as new, and desire to secure by Letters Patent, is—

1. In a condensation-displacement lubricator for multiple-expansion engines, the combination with the sight-feed tubes, of pipes or passages leading therefrom to the high and low pressure cylinders, respectively, and an auxiliary steam-pipe leading at its lower end into the pipe or passage from the sight-feed to the lower-pressure cylinder, and independent of the pipe leading to the high-pressure cylinder and at its upper end communicating with the main steam-pipe at a suitable point, substantially as described.

2. In a condensation-displacement lubricator for multiple-expansion engines, the combination with the sight-feed tubes each having an independent connection with the oil-reservoir, of pipes leading therefrom to the high and low pressure cylinders, respectively, and an auxiliary steam-pipe leading at its lower end into the pipe from the sight-feed to the lower-pressure cylinder, and independent of the pipe leading to the high-pressure cylinder and at its upper end communicating with the main steam-pipe at a suitable point, substantially as described.

3. In a condensation-displacement lubricator for multiple-expansion engines, the combination with the sight-feed tubes, of independent pipes leading therefrom to the main steam-pipe and to the intermediate and low pressure cylinders, respectively, and independent auxiliary steam-pipes, one for each of the pipes leading to the intermediate and low pressure cylinders, connecting with said pipes at their lower ends and at their upper ends communicating with the main steam-pipe at any suitable point above the point of introduction thereinto of the oil for the high-pressure cylinder, substantially as described.

4. In a lubricator for multiple-expansion engines, the combination with the oil-feed passage into the main steam-pipe for the lubricant for the high-pressure cylinder, and an oil-feed pipe leading to each of the other cylinders, of an independent auxiliary steam pipe or pipes, one for each of said last-named feed-pipes, which auxiliary pipes communicate at the upper end with the main steam-pipe at a suitable point, and at their lower ends lead into the respective feed-pipes, substantially as described.

5. In a condensation-displacement lubricator for multiple-expansion engines, the combination with the sight-feed tubes, of feed-pipes, one for conveying oil into the main steam-pipe for the high-pressure cylinder, and another for conveying oil from the other sight-feed to the low-pressure cylinder, and a pipe for the water of condensation leading upwardly from the oil-reservoir into the bottom of a condensing-chamber connected with the main steam-pipe, and an auxiliary steam-pipe connecting at its upper end into the upper part of the condensing-chamber and at its lower end into the oil-feed pipe to the low-pressure cylinder and independent of the oil-feed pipe to the high-pressure cylinder, substantially as described.

6. In a condensation-displacement lubricator for multiple-expansion engines, the combination with two cylinders of different pressures, of an oil-reservoir, two independent oil-feed pipes for conducting oil from the reservoir to said cylinders respectively, and two independent auxiliary steam-pipes communicating with said oil-feed pipes, respectively, substantially as described.

In testimony whereof I have signed this specification in the presence of two subscribing witnesses.

ELIJAH McCOY.

Witnesses:
J. G. EDWARDS,
M. H. WILLIAMS.

UNITED STATES DEPARTMENT OF COMMERCE NEWS

WASHINGTON, D.C. 20230

OFFICE
OF THE
SECRETARY

FOR IMMEDIATE RELEASE WEDNESDAY, JULY 9, 1969

REMARKS BY THE HONORABLE MAURICE H. STANS,
SECRETARY OF COMMERCE, AT NEWS CONFERENCE,
WEDNESDAY, JULY 9, 1969

It is our purpose today to make some major announcements for the Office of

Minority Business Enterprise which, we feel, will make a major contribution to

the goal of giving minority group members a piece of the economic action . . . .

As you know, the President last March signed the executive order creating

the Office within the Commerce . . . Department.

Since then the new office, headed by Tom Roeser and his deputy, Abe Venable,

has been developing a national strategy for minority business which enlists the

private, independent and public sectors . . .

Black Capitalism:

Invention and Innovation as a Vital New American Force

This chapter is an outline of the new look in entrepreneurship for these United States. Concluding the chapter are several pages of "Statistics in Ebony" . . . that will furnish the "background lighting" for this new era.

The principal source of these particular statistics is the United States Department of Commerce; indeed, this organization issued the "press release" excerpts which appear on the opposite page. The author has included this specific item because it illustrateses the broad, national scope of a new and powerful social force — a large and growing black middle class made up of professionals, educators, government employees, and private business owners or entrepreneurs.

An *invention*, together with its *patent,* is an "economical property." It is of great interest to determine just how well the black inventor and innovator himself is faring on today's business and industrial state. Black capitalism has been variously referred to as "a form of black power" . . . "Green power for the ghetto" . . . "the economics of liberation" . . ., etc. It is easier to define in terms of what's happening, in the form of on-going daily programs, than it is to analyze the "rhetoric of freedom," with its highly emotional content.

The motivations are easily understood and arise directly from *social* and *political* situations which were outlined in the introduction. The following ratios are cited in order to furnish additional "backlighting" for our stage: In 1969, blacks made up fully 50 percent of the population of Newark, New Jersey, yet held only 9 percent of the business licenses! At the same time, Los Angeles had 600,000 blacks and 121,039 licensed businesses, but of these, blacks owned less than 1 percent! And solely within the environs of the ghetto itself, 98 percent of the businesses were owned by *whites . . . who did not reside there.* Similar ratios held true for the rest of urban America.

In the 1960s, there came into being at least a score of organizations, movements, corporations, government and municipal programs, and other vehicles — all with the avowed goal of "freeing the black man from his economic plantation." Many have had remarkable success and some have long since been forgotten.

Still, it is not the purpose of this book to provide a critical analysis; but, rather, to focus attention upon the resurgence of that 19th century phenomena of invention and innovation.

The movement is not without its problems; some of them forged upon the bitterest of ironies. After some success in the struggle for equal employment opportunities, black leaders now find a new obstacle to overcome. At the same time that many blacks are permitted to perform the very skills and managerial functions vital to proprietorship (for white employers), the black employee has great difficulty in "spinning off," like other Americans . . . primarily because of the racial barriers to obtaining long-term leaseholds, franchises, distributorships, "paper discount," etc. Obviously, much of the money, talent, and energy available for normal operations must be expanded to overcome *cultural inertia.*

The movement is not without its humor, as witness the fact that some black corporate chiefs were beginning to refer to black personnel agency operators as "black headhunters."

This animosity stems from a very strong suspicion that the big corporate clients of these agencies are able to out-bid them for the cream of the bright, black, college crop. In order to satisfy government contract compliance regulations and other legislation against job discrimination. What began only in firms contracting with the federal government became — with the introduction of affirmative action regulations — a necessity for nearly all companies of any size and all governmental agencies. It is a fact that qualified blacks often earn more than whites because businesses are hard-pressed to employ sufficient minorities. Unfortunately, this most often benefits educated blacks who are already in the higher income levels

Another significant development is that following the blacks' lead, lower income whites are rapidly adopting the same techniques. Again, unfortunately, legislative mandates only affect a small number of those it is intended to serve, and may be rescinded when political climates change. They cannot replace the independence and security of economic strength gained through individual and group innovation and perseverance.

History Again

Here again, we must underscore the controlling events of the 19th century. The end of the Civil War found the black man *with many resources for the vigorous pursuit of his economic welfare* — resources not now commonly available to him. The two absolute essentials for expansion of an economic base were present: a high concentration of *crafts* and *skills*; and the availability of *land*, either in the immediate vicinity or lying to the west. As mentioned earlier, he had a virtual monopoly on such basic crafts as carpentry, masonry, metalworking, carriage making, plumbing, railroad construction, etc. — plus the business experience gained in non-slave areas of the South. Too, when the slave masters discovered the mechanical and computing abilities we have documented, he was impressed into additional activities, such as storekeeping, dock and wharf maintenance, and machine maintenance.

We have further seen that the black man launched what should have been one of the *greatest feats of economic engineering ever performed by man* . . . primarily derived from the psychological impact of *"newly achieved freedom."* However, instead of this natural and logical course of events, the black man fell before what was probably the greatest onslaught of physical violence and legal repression ever before inflicted upon "free men." This annihilative effect was further intensified by the rapid increase of European immigration.

It must be noted that tens of thousands of white, laboring-class workers tried, against insuperable odds, to include the black man . . . in both union and political affairs; but all fell before the onslaught of the Klan, anti-Unionism, and, finally, with the demise of the Populist Party, at the turn of the century. *It was only then that a great number of Southern states enacted the poll taxes and the repressive "Jim Crow" laws.*

In 1886, the National Labor Union asked Isaac Meyers, foremost black labor leader of both Craft and Unskilled Black Workers, . . . to join their ranks; but the blacks refused the "Jim Crow Locals" and established their own "National Colored Labor

Union," which accepted *both races*. However, the Mineworkers, Tobacco Unions, Dock and Cotton Council, and many Longshoremen Groups resisted the growing racism and admitted all races, for decades. These events both help to shape and ameliorate the probably success of today's black capitalism.

Even earlier, however, a process of attrition gnawed at the ranks of black businessmen and capitalists. Where before there had been many wealthy black planters, like the father of sugar engineer Rillieux and the astute Senator Bruce . . . and where both Northern and Southern court records detail innumerable instances of litigation that was initiated by or against black merchants, brokers, shippers, etc., . . . and where Europeans returned from America to write of blacks who had amassed "fortunes in trade" . . . nevertheless, the end of the Civil War found their number more than *halved.*[4]

Thus, the black capitalist inherited a fragmented, frustrated, and disillusioned human resource. Because of the craft union barriers that were erected, training is lacking even in the very fields where *the black man set such fantastic standards. Even today, his buildings, mansions, docks, iron works, water and sewage systems, etc. . . . still stand and are in use in many parts of the South — after as much as two hundred years.*

Consequent psychological damage, over a hundred-year period, presents the black capitalist with personality factors that impede new organization and program implementation; so much so that, until recently, many blacks, as unaware of their historical background as most whites, refused to be associated with, or even *respect*, an institution with a black "aura."

On the other side of the balance sheet is what may prove to be the greatest and most productive asset possessed by the black capitalist; that is, for structuring a *third renaissance*, which could leave the other two *pale by comparison*. We refer here to the new, dynamic sense of "*identity*" that is gripping an aggressive and volatile generation of black youth. Black entrepreneurs are able to project a programming of

---

4   For a definitive treatment of the "Philadelphia Story," where desenfranchisement reduced the roster of black tradesmen from 344 in 1838 to 111 in 1849, see E. P. Foley, *Daedalus,* Winter 1966.

this ingenious and courageous talent . . . in combination with the older, *racially* experienced (and *economically* experienced) black who is *"mentally emancipated."*

Some of these "integrated packages" are already producing startling results. Hundreds of new corporations are springing up around the country, in such fields as plastic manufacturing, computer service bureaus, foundries, banks, bus companies, shopping centers, electronic firms, etc. A contributing factor is that beginning with the "Civil Rights" and "Equal Opportunity" drives of the 1950's, token numbers of blacks, necessarily better educated than their peer groups, began to find admittance to industry at the engineering and managerial levels previously denied to them. Now, many of these seasoned veterans are beginning to "spin-off" and are busy packaging new techniques of manufacturing and marketing.

Again, the black innovator is on his way — once more expecting to *create millions of jobs* and *billions in wealth* for all Americans! (We doubt, if they, like the chemist, Dr. Carver, intend to create entire industries and then find that their sons may only be menials and their daughters barred even from office jobs.) Also, in his favor is a fact substantiated in this text: *the black engineers and system builders are there!* — with or without college training!

The new black managers know that . . . if a hundred years ago, black grammar school drop-outs could *conceive, design,* and *manufacture* the most complicated types of industrial machinery . . . surely they have access today to a *multi-billion dollar* gold mine of *tens of thousands* of talented black innovators.

Many, like the author, are working 16 hours a day to develop devices and software for teaching calculus and analytic geometry down to the Montessori level; devising computer program simulators for third graders and housewives; replicas of communication systems which will simultaneously combine the technique with an exposition of linear programming.

Other blacks have spun out of the aerospace industry . . . to set up shop where they can engineer, improvise, and invent, unfettered by archaic concepts . . . predicated upon culture, race, or the hundred years' rewriting of history.

Some are working on transportation and urban-planning concepts that are a century advanced over anything other Americans have yet conceived. As a matter of fact, the 1969-1970 period will see a number of regional and national "Black Inventor Fairs."

Pertinent information on many such activities may be obtained from the United States Department of Commerce, Office of Minority Business Enterprise; Washington, D. C. 20230.

Things to look for from Black engineering of the future:

... for fire engines and allied apparatus to become oddities (if not obsolete entirely) as both conventional and forest fires are snuffed out by combustion-arresting sound generators;

... for the already-functioning black computer services to "scale down" their services for housewives, students, and even the man-in-the-street — personalized services that are undreamed of at present;

... for radically new means of *capitalizing* and *financing* the "little guy" — with housewives and students "underwriting" equipment trust certificates; in short, for new forms of capitalism;

... for eventual success from the Los Angeles black man, now working in his garage ... on a continuous process machine that takes "paper," conveniently stored in liquid form, and combines it (in its transition to sheets) with the electrostatic output of "copy," stored in magnetic disk form. Output: push-button production of books, newspapers, etc. — to order. (But surely this is not too difficult for men who could design automatic shoemaking machinery a hundred years ago!)

Where the Action is Today

The "Sullivan Complexes," begun by the Reverend Leon Sullivan, Pastor of Zion Baptist Church, Philadelphia, Pennsylvania, included shopping centers, vocational training centers, bus companies, business loan corporations, retail stores, apartment projects, aerospace component manufacturing, service industries.

Initially based in Philadelphia, this successful combination of enterprise, training, and financing has expanded, nationwide, in a few short years! There are now branch operations in over seventy cities. One of the most beneficial "spin-offs" has been the proliferation of *management know-how*. Many similar operations have been founded by skilled Blacks who served their "apprenticeship" in the Sullivan complex.

The key to the successful operations of the dynamic Mr. Sullivan . . . has been his "integrated package technique," in which the combined resources of a city's financial, industrial, and human resource sectors are united. Then, the latent talent and ambition of the frustrated and jobless, the energy of civic leaders, the resources of Federal, state and city government . . . all are pooled and harnessed to the *economic machine!* The result has received world-wide acclaim . . . for here, in its essence, is the execution of a large project where, for a change, it is supported by thorough planning, adequate funding, and an "involved" public sector.

In July of 1969, the U. S. Department of Commerce announced that Reverend Sullivan had been jointly granted by its Economic Development Administration and its Small Business Administration . . . $650,000, to send trained "shopping center developers" to thirteen cities. In each of these major metropolitan areas, these black managerial specialists were to put together a dynamic package of . . . sites, financing and the contracting commitments necessary for the establishment of centers, similar to the original operation in Philadelphia.

Major Government officials participating in this new development (as announced as a special news conference) were Secretary of Commerce, Maurice H. Stans; Administrator Hilary Sandoval, of the Small Business Administration; the Director of the Office of Minority Business Enterprise, Tom Roeser; and the Deputy Director, Abe Venable.

California Special: "The Watts Industrial Park"

This brilliantly conceived vehicle for Black economic development was a black-managed industrial complex . . . located *in the heart of one of the world's greatest industrial centers.* It was established to "develop maximum new employment opportunities"; to "create new business within the area, with special emphasis on local ownership and management"; and, of course, to carry out most of the conventional, if less innovative, functions of these objectives.

The initial "Forty Acres" was assembled by the Economic Resources Corporation and some criteria for tenancy follow:

> Hiring policy must conform with current fair employment legislation with particular concern given to offering employment on all levels of people from the immediate surrounding community.

Tenancy must represent expansion and new employment. It must not cause loss or displacement of existing employees.

The potential work force must exceed a ratio of one employee to every 317 square feet in facility.

The level of training must develop skills which will give employee job mobility, as well as opportunities for advancement.

Firms must be creditworthy of long-term (20-25 years) lease agreements.

The Albina Corporation

In an evergreen land of vast hydroelectric complexes, the "Albina" approach was initially conceived by Mr. Linus J. Niedermeyer, a successful Portland (Oregon) businessman. Early in 1967, Mr. Niedermeyer, impressed especially with the development of the Watts Manufacturing Company of Los Angeles, a "ghetto subsidiary" of the Aerojet Corporation, decided to attempt a similar subsidiary in the Albina District of Portland, Oregon.

Subsequent conversations with community leaders and residents, as well as observation of the problems experienced by similarly based subsidiaries, led Mr. Niedermeyer to believe that such a project would be more meaningful if owned and operated by the Black residents of the community. With the assistance and guidance of the Portland Metropolitan Steering Committee, the local Community Action Agency, and the Albina Citizens' War of Poverty Committee, a neighborhood OEO group, a plan, and organizational structure for the proposed corporation were developed.

Initially supervised by a Board of Directors comprised of thirteen members representing various organizations active in community-improvement projects, the Albina Corporation came into physical being in early May, 1968, when it acquired a 27,000 square foot production and training site in Portland, along with a $195,525 MA-3 contract with the United States Department of Labor for manpower training. Additional grants and contracts from the Federal Government's Office of Economic Opportunity, Small Business Administration, and other agencies brought the Corporation's initial capitalization close to one million dollars.

The Albina Corporation's first President was Clifford J. Campbell, Jr. Its new President and Board Chairman is Attorney Mayfield K. Webb, a black "prime mover."

This is now the "Albina" method works. Two related organizations — each based on a sound economic concept and designed to complement the other — are responsible for carrying out the unique "Albina" approach. One is The Albina Corporation, a profit-making metal and plastic manufacturing company, located in the Albina District of Portland, Oregon, of whom the management staff and employees are drawn from the residents of the Albina Community.

The other is the Albina Investment Trust, a deferred compensation trust established in behalf of the employees of the Albina Corporation, which owns the majority interest in the Corporation and is responsible for educating the employees in capital ownership.

The Second Income Plan (S.I.P.), administered jointly by the Albina Corporation and the Albina Investment Trust, stipulated that the Corporation will pay into the Trust, on behalf of each of its employees, 15 percent of his total annual compensation at the end of each year. While the Albina Investment Trust is responsible for the education of the Corporation's employees in capital ownership, the Albina Corporation, the profit-making company, provides and operates manufacturing facilities for training its employees in a series of sophisticated modern industrial skills. Employees, drawn from among the economically disadvantaged residents of the Albina Community, thus acquired industrial skills while earning a living, and advancing to capital ownership, while creating other opportunities of economic development for their community.

The author gives a lecture/demonstration in communications and related mathematics/data processing at a junior high school in The Dalles, Oregon. A 'resource" person from the accounting department of a local aluminum company at the time, Burt later "invented" his own business: A "rolling" communications van employing his own inventions for teaching and analoging the associated math/programming. (1966)

Statistics In Ebony

The 1960 Census records a total of 18.8 million black people and the most recent estimate (1985) is 29 million; 13.6 million males and 15.2 million females. This is 12.1 percent of the population and that percentage should continue to *increase*, because 15 percent of the children under five are black. Birth rates have been declining for both blacks and the general population since 1957; however, while the birth rate was 16.7 babies per thousand population for whites — in 1967 — it 25.4 for blacks. Significantly, by 1985, the white birth rate had declined nearly 12% to 14.7, but the black rate declined even faster, 16.9%, to 21.1. Both rates are projected to continue this trend through the end of the century.

In the days of slavery and for many years afterward, most of us lived on farms. At the turn of the century 80 percent of our people still were in the rural areas. But farming changed. Machines began to replace people on the farms. We had to move to new places, to new kinds of work. By 1940, only about a third of us lived on farms; by 1960 the proportion was down to 8 percent, and by 1970, 4.8%. Now it is about 3 percent or less, about the same percentage as for the white population.

Where did we go? Most of us, perhaps after several moves, wound up in the cities — in the big cities. From 1950 to 1968, the total black population increased by 7 million, and 5 million of the increase was in the central cities of our metropolitan areas. More than half (54 percent) of us now live inside the central cities. So, starting out as "farm" people, we have now become "big-city" people.

The whites, too, moved from farms to the cities, and then on to the suburbs. Considering only the metropolitan areas, most of the blacks are in the central cities and most of the whites are in the suburbs. The most recent figures indicate an increase

Black Urban Population Change

	1960			1985		
	Black Population	Percent Black	Rank	Black Population	Percent Black	Rank
New York	1,087,931	14	1	1,911,525	23.1	1
Chicago	812,637	23	2	1,352,380	22.3	2
Detroit	482,223	29	4	893,112	19.9	3
Philadelphia	529,240	26	3	886,796	18.8	4
Washington DC	411,737	54	5	871,268	26.8	5
Los Angeles	334,916	14	6	842,228	12.6	6
Baltimore	325,589	35	7	561,000	25.5	7
Atlanta	186,464	38	12	525,948	24.6	8
Houston	215,037	23	10	514,368	18.8	9
New Orleans	233,514	37	9	409,456	32.6	10
St Louis	214,377	29	11	408,844	17.2	11
Newark	138,035	34	14	407,743	21.7	12
Memphis	184,320	37	13	364,287	39.9	13
Cleveland	250,818	29	8	345,618	18.2	14
Norfolk	78,806	26	24	325,960	28.1	15
Dallas	129,242	19	16	315,077	16.1	16
Miami	65,213	22	31	279,672	17.2	17
Oakland	83,618	23	21	264,300	15.0	18
Birmingham	135,118	4	15	240,448	27.2	19
Richmond	91,972	42	20	221,451	29.1	20
Kansas City MO	83,146	18	22	180,558	12.6	21
Cincinnati	108,754	22	17	173,724	12.4	22
Pittsburgh	100,692	17	18	170,863	7.7	23
Boston	63,165	9	33	162,748	5.8	24
Indianapolis	98,049	21	19	157,545	13.5	25
Jacksonville	82,525	41	23	155,952	21.6	26
Milwaukee	62,458	8	34	150,876	10.8	27
Nashville	64,570	28	32	137,011	16.1	28
Columbus	77,140	16	25	136,840	11.0	29
San Francisco	74,383	1	26	128,054	8.6	30
Mobile	65,619	32	30	126,984	28.6	31
Gary	69,123	39	29	126,671	19.7	32
Louisville	70,075	18	28	120,582	12.6	33
Buffalo	70,904	13	27	102,515	10.1	34

in the number of blacks in the central cities and a slight increase in our suburban population since 1960.

Let's take another look at our long-term movement. As we moved from the farm to the city, we also moved from the South to the North and West. In 1860, our population was four and a half million including four million slaves. At that time 92 percent of all black Americans lived in the South. In 1900, 90 percent of us were still there; but then we began to spread out. By 1940 the census showed just 77 percent of us in the South. By 1960 this figure was down to 60 percent and the 1968 estimate was 53 percent. The Census Bureau counts Maryland, Delaware, Kentucky, Oklahoma, West Virginia and the District of Columbia as "South" along with the States of the old Confederacy.

Looking to the future, the Census Bureau says that there probably will be about 31 million black Americans by 1990 and more than 35 million by 2000. We will account for 12.4 percent of the total population in 1990 and 13.6 percent by 1990.

The black labor force is expected to increase by almost four million from 1985 to 2000, while the total labor force will be adding 10 million. The nation will need to find two additional jobs for every ten held by blacks in 1985.

The average black family earns less money than the average white family, although the average black family is larger. Nine percent of the families in the United States are black, but we receive only five percent of the national income. Our pay is lowest in the South and highest in the West and Midwest. The income gap between whites and blacks follows the same pattern . . . widest in the South and narrower in the West and the Midwest.

Black median income was 59 percent of the median income for white families in 1967, 60.8% in 1970, dropped to 57.6% in 1980 and other recessionary years following, and rebounded to 59.5% in 1985.

One reason our incomes are so low is that black families are three times as likely to be headed by a woman as white families. Of even greater note, however, is that half of us still live in the South, where the cost of living — and incomes — fall below the national average. Also affecting these averages are the ages of the respective groups. The median age for whites is 32, but the median age for blacks is only 26. This means that a much greater percentage of our population is not even out of school, and the average black employee has *at least six years less work experience* than his or her white counterpart.

With such a large part of our population not in the workforce, lacking as much experience, or concentrated in the South, *average* income figures are difficult to accurately compare with the national average. On the other hand, renowned black economists Thomas Sowell (Senior Fellow, Hoover Institution, Stanford University) and Walter Williams (Professor of Economics, George Mason University) have pointed out that if we compare white and black workers of the same age, who live in the same part of the country, and have the same educational background and similar jobs, we earn 94 percent of what whites do.

Finally, our low income level is caused by our having so many low-paying jobs. About two of every five black men and more than half of all black women who work are service workers, laborers, or farm workers.

But we are growing away from these low-paying jobs. A comparison of 1960 and 1967 employment figures shows that 169,000 fewer blacks worked in household service, 70,000 fewer were laborers, and 453,000 fewer worked on farms in 1967. At the same time, the number of black professional, technical, and crafts workers increased by about 1.4 million.

Black representation in the professions and in some skill areas remains proportionately small, although it has improved markedly during the past two decades. Blacks represent 9.8 percent of the workforce in this country, but only 3.7 percent of the doctors (although this has almost doubled, from 2%, in 1967), 2.6 percent of the dentists, 4.7 percent of the insurance brokers (up from 1.5% in 1967), 3.3 percent of the plumbers, 8.3 percent of the electricians (also up from 1.5%), and 2.6 percent of the engineers (from 0.5%). We also make up 3.3 percent of the lawyers & judges (up from 2.4%), 6.8 percent of registered nurses (5.6%), 6.5 percent of the medical technicians, 2.4 percent of the telephone operators, and 6.5 percent of the secretaries (1.3%).

We have our full share of some jobs, including clergymen (12.6%), social workers (17.6%), data entry typists (19.5%), teachers' aides (17.8%), mail carriers (19.8%), postal clerks (26.1%), cosmetologists, and dietitians. And we have more than our share of masons, metal workers, plasterers, service station attendants, furnace men, laundry workers, packers, taxi-drivers, elevator operations, and practical nurses (19.6%). We are over-represented in law enforcement, with 13.5 percent of the jobs, and elementary school teachers (11.1%, up from 8.8%) and vocational and educational counselors (11.7%).

Some of us are self-employed: 178,000 with farms, 1,200 with clothing stores, 400 with furniture stores, 2,600 with gasoline and service stations, 300 with household appliance stores, over 8,000 with trucking services, 4,000 in wholesale trade, 13,000 with food and dairy stores, 15,000 with eating and drinking places, and 1,700 with other retail stores of various kinds.

There is some black ownership of almost every conceivable kind of enterprise from hotels and radio stations to banks, management consultant firms, and supermarkets.

Unemployment is still a major problem for black Americans, although the employment statistics are more encouraging now than in earlier years. An estimated 638,000 blacks were unemployed in 1967. Matters became worse during the 70s and 80s, with unemployment peaking at 2.2 million in 1983 and declining rapidly to 1.8 million in 1985. This corresponds to a total unemployment rate of 7.4% in 1967, 19.5% in 1983, and 15.1% in 1985. Compared with white workers, we are twice as likely to be out of work.

On the other hand, the number of working blacks has increased from 8.9 to 12.3 million between 1973 and 1985 — *an increase of more than 2.4 million jobs*. Unfortunately, in the same period, 3.3 million of us entered the prospective workforce.

But in urban ghetto areas the problem is the worst, with one out of every three available black workers either unemployed of seriously underemployed — that is, working for substandard pay or working only part-time. Nationally, 14 percent of our people are on welfare, compared with three percent of whites.

Both the employment and welfare figures could improve if we can raise the educational level of our children . . . and our educational record looks better every year, with fewer dropouts and more high school graduates and college students. Only 12.9 percent of our young completed four years of high school in 1960. But by 1970 that figure had risen to 21.1 percent, and in 1980 and 1985 the figures further improved to 29.3 and 33.9 percent. And although the proportion of young adults who have completed high school continues to rise for both races, the gap between black and white has narrowed sharply. While the graduation rate for whites was 25.8 percent in 1960, it increase more slowly to 39 percent in 1985. Thus, while the white graduation rate rose 51%, *our* graduation rate rose *163 percent*.

Over 40 percent of our families own their own homes — an increase from 24 percent in 1940. However, much of the housing we live in is substandard. Three of every ten dwellings occupied by black families are dilapidated or lack hot water, a toilet, tub or shower.

Almost half (46 percent) of the black people in the South and 16 percent of those in the North and West live in such housing. Slowly these substandard housing units are disappearing. The number of black-occupied housing units described as dilapidated or lacking basic plumbing declined from 2.2 million in 1960 to 1.7 million in 1966. The number of whites in such housing is even greater (declining from 6.2 million to 4 million), but because their total population is much greater, the percentage that represents is much smaller.

We are buying more and more automobiles and appliances. By the late 1960s about 52 percent of our families had at least one car; 10 percent owned two or more. Eighty-nine percent owned television sets, seventy-six percent of us had refrigerators or freezers, 4 percent had dishwashers, and 8 percent owned room air conditioners. Although new census data were not available at publication, all of these figures have shown substantial improvement during the past two decades.

In 1967, there were 303,000 blacks in the Armed Forces, or 9 percent of the total. This included 10 percent of the troops in Southeast Asia.

Although we made up 9 percent of the armed forces, only 2 percent of all officers were black. On December 31, 1967, there were 8,000 black officers including 1,000 in Vietnam. Of the 295,000 black enlisted men, 55 thousand were in Vietnam. by 1985, however, there were 404,600 of us in the military, or 18.9% of the total, including 19,800 officers (a *148%* increase, 3,700 of them black *women*). We were still under-represented here, with only 6.4% of the total officers.

But General Colin Powell has been quoted as saying that his race has never posed an obstacle to his career in the Army.

Nevertheless, in spite of our under-representation among college graduates, from whom many officers are drawn, our representation in the officer' corps grew faster than did our percentage in the military as a whole. There have even been black astronauts chosen to perform complex and expensive operations in space — some costing tens of millions of dollars. In 1990, President George Bush appointed General

Powell to the post of Chairman of the Joint Chiefs of Staff, the highest position in the military service.[5] As America's most powerful soldier, he is responsible only to the Secretary of Defense and the President.

Between 1970 and 1986, the number of black elected officials increased from 1,479 to 6,312. 407 of us are members of the U.S. Congress or state legislatures, 3,689 hold elective office in city and county governments, 685 in law enforcement, and 1,531 in state education agencies, college boards, and school boards. Some of us are, or have been, Mayor of major cities like Los Angeles, New York, Chicago, Atlanta, and Cleveland. In 1988, Jesse Jackson — although not chosen — was seriously considered as a candidate for Vice President of the United States, and in 1990 Douglas Wilder was elected Governor of Virginia, in an election most observers agreed was decided purely on the issues, not on the race of the candidates.[6]

To sum up, we are in many ways still not where we would like to be, but our lot has improved. Since *Black Inventors* was first published, our representation in jobs with greater responsibility — and higher pay — has improved notably, sometimes even remarkably. The improvements are not always big and obvious, and setbacks are common . . . but they are real, and they will never be taken away from us. As we succeed in preparing our children, with better education, and superior work habits and attitudes, we see changes in the attitudes of others toward us. In many states and cities, white voters are choosing *us* to represent *them* — to govern *their* lives. As our children grow up to live and work in such a world, there is no limit to what their imaginations can invent.

---

5   For more information about this subject, see *Black Americans in Defense of Their Nation,* National Book, 1991.

6   For more information about this subject, see *Black Americans in Politics, Volume 1: Black Americans in Congress,* National Book, 1991.)

W. J. Knickerson
(attachment)
June 26, 1899
#627,739

P. B. Downing
October 27, 1891
#462,096 & #462,093

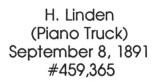

H. Linden
(Piano Truck)
September 8, 1891
#459,365

I. R. Johnson, Bicycle Frame
October 10, 1899, #634,823

A. J. Polk, Holder for Bicycle
april 14, 1896, #558,103

W. Murray, Attachment for Bicycle
January 27, 1891, #445,452

W. Johnson, Velocipede
June 20, 1899, #627,335

J. B. Rhodes
December 19, 1899
#639,290

J. L. Love
(Pencil Sharpener)
November 23, 1897
#594,114

Appendix

The Unfinished Declaration of Independence of the United States

The final version of the Declaration of Independence (as accepted by the Congress) did not include the following paragraph, which was written by Thomas Jefferson as part of the initial draft of the document.

> *"He has waged a cruel war against human nature itself, violating its most sacred rights of **life** and **liberty** in the **persons** of a **distant people** who never offended him, captivating and carrying them into slavery in another hemisphere, or to incur miserable death in their transportation thither. This piratical warfare, the opprobrium of infidel powers, is the warfare of the Christian king of Great Britain. Determined to keep open **a market where MEN should be bought and sold,** he has prostituted his negative for suppressing every legislative attempt to prohibit or to restrain this execrable commerce; and that this assemblage of horrors might want no fact of distinguished die, he is now exciting these very people to rise in arms among us, and to purchase that liberty of which he deprived them, by murdering the people upon whom he also obtruded them; thus paying off former crimes committed against the liberties of one people, with crimes which he urges them to commit against the lives of another."*

It is probably true that the omission of this paragraph reflected an acute awareness on the part of certain congressmen that some influential New England merchants were profitably engaged in the slave trade. There were other legislators who were simply in favor of slavery and sensed that the inclusion of such a paragraph would prejudice the case for its continuation.

The Patent Process

The first patent act in the United States was signed by George Washington, in 1790, with only three patents being granted during the first year. Between 1961 and 1970 more than 618,000 patents were issued, and 731,000 were issued during the 1970s. By 1986, 77,000 patents a year were being issued. The first patent known to have been granted to a black man was issued to Henry Blair, of Maryland, for a cornplanting machine.

A patent lasts 17 years. Fundamentals of the patent system are, in general, that any person who has invented any new, useful, novel process; new machine, manufacturing process, or composition of matter; and also certain varieties of plants, or improvements thereto, . . . may obtain a patent!

The first condition requires that the invention must not have been previously patented or described in any printed publication in any country, or in public use, or on sale in *this* country. The second condition stipulates that the invention be operative for a useful purpose. (In early days it was necessary to have constructed a "working" model . . . See heading of Actual Patent Applications in this book, for earlier periods.) The third condition recites the degree of ingenuity or cleverness needed to warrant a patent: It must be "*unobvious*" to the "*skilled*" person in the art.

Patents are grouped under one or another of some 340 headings. These in turn are broken down into 80,000 subject groups. (Recent new approaches and computerized restructuring of procedures have slightly changed this classification.) There are three broad, "generic" divisions of patents: mechanical, design, and reissue. However, 90 percent of patents granted come under the heading of *mechanical*, and have a life of *17 years*. Design patents refer generally to novel and ingenious appearances . . . such as furniture, lampshades, fabric patterns, shoe styles, and the decorations on dishes. Such design patents may be obtained for terms of *3½, 7, or 14* years.

Patent and Invention Index

Inventor	Invention	Date	Patent
Abrams, W. B.	Hame Attachment	Apr. 14, 1891	450,550
Allen, C. W.	Self-Leveling Table	Nov. 1, 1898	613,436
Allen, J. B.	Clothes Line Support	Dec. 10, 1895	551,105
Ashbourne, A. P.	Process Preparing Coconut for Domestic Use	June 1, 1875	163,962
Ashbourne, A. P.	Biscuit Cutter	Nov. 30, 1875	170,460
Ashbourne, A. P.	Refining Coconut Oil	July 27, 1880	230,518
Ashbourne, A. P.	Process of Treating Coconut	Aug. 21, 1877	194,287
Bailes, Wm.	Ladder Scaffold-Support	Aug. 5, 1879	218,154
Bailey, L. C.	Combined Truss and Bandage	Sept. 25, 1883	285,545
Bailey, L. C.	Folding Bed	July 18, 1899	629,286
Bailiff, C. O.	Shampoo Headrest	Oct. 11, 1898	612,008
Ballow, W. J.	Combined Hatrack and Table	Mar. 29, 1898	601,422
Barnes, G. A. E.	Design for Sign	Aug. 19, 1898	29,193
Beard, A. J.	Car Coupler	Nov. 23, 1897	594,059
Beard, A. J.	Rotary Engine	July 5, 1892	478,271
Becket, G. E.	Letter Box	Oct. 4, 1892	483,325
Bell, L.	Locomotive Smoke Stack	May 23, 1871	115,153
Bell, L.	Dough Kneader	Dec 10, 1872	133,823
Benjamin, L. W.	Broom Moisteners and Bridles	May 16, 1893	497,747
Benjamin, M. E.	Gong and Signal Chairs for Hotels	July 17, 1888	386,286
Binga, M. W.	Street Sprinkling Apparatus	July 22, 1879	217,843
Blackburn, A. B.	Railway Signal	Jan 10, 1888	376,362
Blackburn, A. B.	Spring Seat for Chairs	Apr. 3, 1888	380,420
Blackburn, A. B.	Cash Carrier	Oct. 23, 1888	391,577
Blair, Henry	Corn Planter	Oct. 14, 1834	— -
Blair, Henry	Cotton Planter	Aug. 31 1836	— -
Blue, L.	Hand Corn Shelling Device	May 20, 1884	298,937
Booker, L. F.	Design Rubber Scraping Knife	Mar. 28, 1899	30,404
Boone, Sarah	Ironing Board	Apr. 26, 1892	473,653
Bowman, H. A.	Making Flags	Feb. 23, 1892	469,395
Brooks, C. B.	Punch	Oct. 31, 1893	507,672
Brooks, C. B.	Street Sweepers	Mar. 17, 1896	556,711
Brooks, C. B.	Street Sweepers	May 12, 1896	560,154
Brooks, Hallstead/Page	Street Sweepers	Apr. 21, 1896	558,719
Brown, Henry	Receptacle for Storing and Preserving Papers	Nov. 2, 1886	352,036
Brown, L. F.	Bridle Bit	Oct 25, 1892	484,994
Brown, O. E.	Horseshoe	Aug. 23, 1892	481,271
Brown & Latimer	Water Closets for Railway Cars	Feb. 10, 1874	147,363
Burr, J. A.	Lawn Mower	May 9, 1899	624,749
Burr, W. F.	Switching Device for Railways	Oct. 31, 1899	636,197
Burwell, W.	Boot or Shoe	Nov. 28, 1899	638,143
Butler, R. A.	Train Alarm	June 15, 1897	584,540
Butts, J. W.	Luggage Carrier	Oct. 10, 1899	634,611

Byrd, T. J.	Improvement in Holders for Reins for Horses	Feb. 6, 1872	123,328
Byrd, T. J.	Apparatus Detaching Horses from Carriages	Mar. 19, 1872	124,790
Byrd, T. J.	Improvement in Neck Yokes for Wagons	Apr. 30, 1872	126,181
Byrd, T. J.	Improvement in Car Couplings	Dec. 1, 1874	157,370
Campbell, W. S.	Self-Setting Animal Trap	Aug. 30, 1881	246,369
Cargill, B. F.	Invalid Cot	July 25, 1899	629,658
Carrington, T. A.	Range	July 25, 1876	180,323
Carter, W. C.	Umbrella Stand	Aug. 4, 1885	323,397
Certain, J. M.	Parcel Carrier for Bicycles	Dec. 26, 1899	639,708
Cherry, M. A.	Velocipede	May 8, 1888	382,351
Cherry, M. A.	Street Car Fender	Jan. 1, 1895	531,908
Church, T. S.	Carpet Beating Machine	July 29, 1884	302,237
Clare, O. B.	Trestle	Oct. 9, 1888	390,753
Coates, R.	Overboot for Horses	Apr. 19, 1892	473,295
Cook, G.	Automatic Fishing Device	May 30, 1899	625,829
Coolidge, J. S.	Harness Attachment	Nov. 13, 1888	392,908
Cooper, A. R.	Shoemaker's Jack	Aug. 22, 1899	631,519
Cooper, J.	Shutter and Fastening	May 1, 1883	276,563
Cooper, J.	Elevator Device	Apr. 2, 1895	536,605
Cooper, J.	Elevator Device	Spe. 21, 1897	590,257
Cornwell, P. W.	Draft Regulator	Oct. 2, 1888	390,284
Cornwell, P. W.	Draft Regulator	Feb. 7, 1893	491,082
Cralle, A. L.	Ice-Cream Mold	Feb. 2, 1897	576,395
Creamer, H.	Steam Feed Water Trap	Mar. 17, 1895	313,854
Creamer, H.	Steam Trap Feeder	Dec. 11, 1888	394,463
(Creamer also patented five steam traps between 1887 and 1893)			
Cosgrove, W. F.	Automatic Stop Plug for Gas Oil Pipes	Mar. 17, 1885	313,993
Darkins, J. T.	Ventilation Aid	Feb 19, 1895	534,322
Davis, I. D.	Tonic	Nov. 2, 1886	351,829
Davis, W. D.	Riding Saddles	Oct. 6, 1896	568,939
Davis, W. R., Jr.	Library Table	Sep. 24, 1878	208,378
Deitz, W. A.	Shoe	Apr. 30, 1867	64,205
Dickinson, J. H.	Pianola	Detroit, Mich. 1899	
Dorsey, O.	Door-Holding Device	Dec. 10, 1878	210,764
Dorticus, C. J.	Device for Applying Coloring Liquids to sides of Soles & Heels of Shoes		
		Mar 19, 1895	535,820
Dorticus, C. J.	Machine for Embossing Photo	Apr. 16, 1895	537,442
Dorticus, C. J.	Photographic Print Wash	Apr. 23, 1895	537,968
Dorticus, C. J.	Hose Leak Stop	July 18, 1899	629,315
Downing, P. B.	Electric Switch for Railroad	June 17, 1890	430,118
Downing, P. B.	Letter Box	Oct. 27, 1891	462.093
Downing, P. B.	Street Letter Box	Oct. 27, 1891	462,096
Dunnington, J. H.	Horse Detachers	Mar. 16, 1897	578,979
Edmonds, T. H.	Separating Screens	July 20, 1897	586,724
Elkins, T.	Dining, Ironing Table and Quilting Frame Combined		
		Feb. 22, 1870	100,020
Elkins, T.	Chamber Commode	Jan 9, 1872	122,518
Elkins, T.	Refrigerating Apparatus	Nov. 4, 1879	221,222
Evans, J. H.	Convertible Settees	Oct. 5, 1897	591,095
Faulkner, H.	Ventilated Shoe	Apr. 29, 1890	426,495
Ferrell, F. J.	Steam Trap	Feb. 11, 1890	420,993
Ferrell, F. J.	Apparatus for Melting Snow	May 27, 1890	428,670

(Ferrell also patented eight valves between 1890 and 1893.)

Fisher, D. A.	Joiner's Clamp	Apr. 20, 1875	162,281
Fisher, D. A.	Furniture Castor	Mar. 14, 1876	174,794
Flemming, R. F., Jr.	Guitar	Mar. 3, 1886	338,727
Forten, J.	Sail Control	Mass. Newspaper 1850	
Goode, Sarah E.	Folding Cabinet Bed	July 14, 1885	322,177
Grant, G. F.	Golf Tee	Dec. 12, 1899	638,920
Grant, W. S.	Curtain Rod Support	Aug. 4, 1896	565,075
Gray, R. H.	Baling Press	Aug. 28, 1894	525,203
Gray, R. H.	Cistern Cleaners	Apr. 9, 1895	537,151
Gregory, J.	Motor	Apr. 26, 1887	361,937
Grenon, H.	Razor Stropping Device	Feb. 18, 1896	554,867
Griffin, F. W.	Pool Table Attachment	June 13, 1899	626,902
Gunn, S. W.	Boot or Shoe	Jan. 16, 1900	641,642
Haines, J. H.	Portable Basin	Sep. 28, 1897	590,833
Hammonds, J. F.	Apparatus for Holding Yarn Skeins	Dec. 15, 1986	572,985
Harding, F. H.	Extension Banquet Table	Nov. 22, 1898	614,468
Hawkins, J.	Gridiron	Mar. 26, 1845	3,973
Hawkins, R.	Harness Attachment	Oct. 4, 1887	370,943
Headen, M.	Foot Power Hammer	Oct. 5, 1886	350,363
Hearness, R.	Sealing Attachment for Bottles	Feb. 15, 1898	598,929
Hearness, R.	Detachable Car Fender	July 4, 1899	628,003
Hilyer, A. F.	Water Evaporator Attachment Hot Air Registers	Aug. 26, 1890	435,095
Hilyer, A. F.	Registers	Oct. 14, 1890	438,159
Holmes, E. H.	Gage	Nov. 12, 1895	549,513
Hunter, J. H.	Portable Weighing Scales	Nov 3, 1896	570,553
Hyde, R. N.	Composition for Cleaning & Preserving Carpets	Nov. 6, 1888	392,205
Jackson, B. F.	Heating Apparatus	Mar. 1, 1898	599,985
Jackson, B. F.	Matrix Drying Apparatus	May 10, 1898	603,879
Jackson, B. F.	Gas Burner	Apr. 4, 1899	622,482
Jackson, H. A.	Kitchen Table	Oct 6, 1896	596,135
Jackson, W. H.	Railway Switch	Mar. 9, 1897	578,641
Jackson, W. H.	Railway Switch	Mar. 16, 1897	593,665
Jackson, W. H.	Automatic Locking Switch	Aug. 23, 1898	609,436
Johnson, D.	Rotary Dining Table	Jan. 15, 1888	396,089
Johnson, D.	Lawn Mower Attachment	Sep. 10, 1889	410,836
Johnson, D.	Grass Receivers for Lawn Mowers	June 10, 1890	429,629
Johnson, I. R.	Bicycle Frame	Oct. 10, 1899	634,823
Johnson, P.	Swinging Chairs	Nov. 15, 1881	249,530
Johnson, P.	Eye Protector	Nov. 2, 1880	234,039
Johnson, W.	Velocipede	June 20, 1899	627,335
Johnson, W. A.	Paint Vehicle	Dec. 4, 1888	393,763
Johnson, W. H.	Overcoming Dead Centers	Feb. 4, 1896	554,223
Johnson, W. H.	Overcoming Dead Centers	Oct. 11, 1898	612,345
Johnson, W.	Egg Beater	Feb. 5, 1884	292,821
Jones, F. M.	Ticket Dispensing Machine	June 27, 1939	2,163,754
Jones, F. M.	Air Conditioning Unit	July 12, 1949	2,475,841
Jones, F. M.	Method for Air Conditioning	Dec. 7, 1954	2,696,086
Jones, F. M.	Method for Preserving Perishables	Feb. 12, 1957	2,780,923
Jones, F. M.	Two-Cycle Gasoline Engine	Nov. 28, 1950	2,523,273
Jones, F. M.	Two-Cycle Gas Engine	May 29, 1945	2,376,968

Jones, F. M.	Starter Generator	July 12, 1949	2,475,842
Jones, F. M.	Starter Generator for Cooling Gas Engines		2,475,843
Jones, F. M.	Two-Cycle Gas Engine	Mar. 11, 1947	2,417,253
Jones, F. M.	Means for Thermostatically Operating Gas Engines	July 26, 1949	2,477,377
Jones, F. M.	Rotary Compressor	Apr. 18, 1950	2,504,841
Jones, F. M.	System for Controlling Operation of Refrigeration Units	May 23, 1950	2,509,099
Jones, F. M.	Apparatus for Heating or Cooling Atmosphere within an Enclosure	Oct 24, 1950	2,526,874
Jones, F. M.	Prefabricated Refrigerator Construction	Dec. 26, 1950	2,535,682
Jones, F. M.	Refrigeration Control Device	Jan. 8, 1952	2,581,956
Jones, F. M.	Methods and Means of Defrosting a Cold Diffuser	Jan. 19, 1954	2,666,298
Jones, F. M.	Control Device for Internal Combustion Engine	Sep. 2, 1958	2,850,001
Jones, F. M.	Thermostat and Temperature Control System	Feb. 23, 1960	2,926,005
Jones, F. M.	Removable Cooling Units for Compartments		2,336,735
Jones, F. M.	Means for Automatically Stopping & Starting Gas Engines ("J. A. Numero et al")	Dec. 21, 1943	2,337,164
Jones, F. M.	Design for Air Conditioning Unit	July 4, 1950	159,209
Jones, F. M.	Design for Air Conditioning Unit	Apr. 28, 1942	132,182
Jones & Long	Caps for Bottles	Sep. 13, 1898	610,715
Joyce, J. A.	Ore Bucket	Apr. 26, 1898	603,143
Latimer & Brown	Water Closets for Railway Cars	Feb. 10, 1874	147,363
Latimer, L. H.	Manufacturing Carbons	June 17, 1882	252,386
Latimer, L. H.	Apparatus for Cooling and Disinfecting	Jan. 12, 1886	334,078
Latimer, L. H.	Locking Racks for Coats, Hats, and Umbrellas	Mar. 24, 1896	557,076
Latimer & Nichols	Electric Lamp	Sep. 13, 1881	247,097
Latimer & Tregoning	Globe Support for Electric Lamps	Mar. 21, 1882	255,212
Lavalette, W. A.	Printing Press	Sep. 17, 1878	208,208
Lee, H	Animal Trap	Feb. 12, 1867	61,941
Lee, J.	Kneading Machine	Aug. 7, 1894	524,042
Lee, J.	Break Crumbing Machine	June 4, 1895	540,553
Leslie, F. W.	Envelope Seal	Sep. 21, 1897	590,325
Lewis, A. L.	Window Cleaner	Sep. 27, 1892	483,359
Lewis, E. R.	Spring Gun	May 3, 1887	362,096
Linden, H.	Piano Truck	Sep. 8, 1891	459,365
Little, E.	Bridle-Bit	Mar. 7, 1882	254,666
Loudin, F. J.	Sash Fastener	Dec. 12, 1892	510,432
Loudin, F. J.	Key Fastener	Jan. 9, 1894	512,308
Love, J. L.	Plasterers' Hawk	July 9, l895	542,419
Love, J. L.	Pencil Sharpener	Nov. 23, 1897	594,114
Marshall, T. J.	Fire Extinguisher	May 26, 1872	125,063
Marshall, W.	Grain Binder	May 11, 1886	341,599
Martin, W. A.	Lock	July 23, 1889	407,738
Martin, W. A.	Lock	Dec. 30, 1890	443,945
Matzeliger, J. E.	Mechanism for Distributing Tacks	Nov. 26, 1899	415,726
Matzeliger, J. E.	Nailing Machine	Feb. 25, 1896	421,954
Matzeliger, J. E.	Tack Separating Mechanism	Mar. 25, 1890	423,937
Matzeliger, J. E.	Lasting Machine	Sep. 22, 1891	459,899
McCoy, E. J.	Lubricator	May 27, 1873	139,407
McCoy, E. J.	Lubricator	Mar. 28, 1882	255,443
McCoy, E. J.	Lubricator	July 18, 1882	261,166

McCoy, E. J.	Lubricator	June 16, 1885	320,379
McCoy, E. J.	Lubricator	Feb. 8, 1887	357,491
McCoy, E. J.	Lubricator	May 29, 1888	383,745
McCoy, E. J.	Lubricator	May 29, 1888	383,746
McCoy, E. J.	Lubricator	Dec. 24, 1899	418,139
McCoy, E. J.	Lubricator	Dec. 29, 1891	465,875
McCoy, E. J.	Lubricator	Apr. 5, 1892	472,066
McCoy, E. J.	Lubricator	Sep. 13, 1898	610,634
McCoy, E. J.	Lubricator	Oct. 4, 1898	611,759
McCoy, E. J.	Oil Cup	Nov. 15, 1898	614,307
McCoy, E. J.	Lubricator	June 27, 1899	627,623
McCoy, E. J.	Lubricator for Steam Engines	July 2, 1872	129,843
McCoy, E. J.	Lubricator for Steam Engines	Aug. 6, 1872	130,305
McCoy, E. J.	Steam Lubricator	Jan. 20, 1874	146,697
McCoy, E. J.	Ironing Table	May 12, 1874	150,876
McCoy, E. J.	Steam Cylinder Lubricator	Feb. 1, 1876	173,032
McCoy, E. J.	Steam Cylinder Lubricator	July 4, 1876	179,585
McCoy, E. J.	Lawn Sprinkler Design	Sep. 26, 1899	631,549
McCoy, E. J.	Steam Dome	June 16, 1885	320,354
McCoy, E. J.	Lubricator Attachment	Apr. 19, 1887	361,435
McCoy, E. J.	Lubricator for Safety Valves	May 24, 1887	363,529
McCoy, E. J.	Drip Cup	Sep. 29, 1891	460,215
McCoy & Hodges	Lubricator	Dec. 24, 1889	418,139
McCree, D.	Portable Fire Escape	Nov. 11, 1890	440,322
Mendenhall, A.	Holder for Driving Reins	Nov. 289, 1899	637,811
Miles, A.	Elevator	Oct. 11, 1887	371,207
Mitchell, C. L.	Phneterisin	Jan. 1, 1884	291,071
Mitchell, J. M.	Cheek Row Corn Planter	Jan. 16, 1900	641,462
Moody, W. U.	Game Board Design	May ll, 1897	27,046
Morehead, K.	Reel Carrier	Oct. 6, 1896	568,916
Murray, G. W.	Combined Furrow Opener and Stalk-Knocker	Apr. 10, 1894	517,960
Murray, G. W.	Cultivator and Marker	Apr. 10, 1894	517,961
Murray, G. W.	Planter	June 5, 1894	520,887
Murray, G. W.	Cotton Chopper	June 5, 1894	520,888
Murray, G. W.	Fertilizer Distributor	June 5, 1894	520,889
Murray, G. W.	Planter	June 5, 1894	520,890
Murray, G. W.	Combined Cotton Seed	June 5, 1894	520,891
Murray, G. W.	Planter and Fertilizer Distributor Reaper	June 5, 1894	520,892
Murray, W.	Attachment for Bicycles	Jan. 27, 1891	445,452
Nance, L.	Game Apparatus	De. 1, 1891	464,035
Nash, H. H.	Life Preserving Stool	Oct. 5, 1875	168,519
Newman, L. D.	Brush	Nov. 15, 1898	614,335
Newson, S.	Oil Heater or Cooker	May 22, 1894	520,188
Nichols & Latimer	Electric Lamp	Sep. 13, 1881	247,097
Nickerson, W. J.	Mandolin and Guitar Attachment for Pianos	June 27, 1899	627,739
O'Connor & Turner	Alarm for Boilers	Aug. 25, 1896	566,612
O'Connor & Turner	Steam Gage	Aug. 25, 1896	566,613
O'Connor & Turner	Alarm for Coasts Containing Vessels	Feb. 8, 1898	598,572
Outlaw, J. W.	Horseshoes	Nov. 15, 1898	614,273
Perryman, F. R.	Caterers' Tray Table	Feb. 2, 1892	468,038
Peterson, H.	Attachment for Lawn Mowers	Apr. 30, 1889	402,189
Phelps, W. H.	Apparatus for Washing Vehicles	Mar. 23, 1897	579,242

Pickering, J. F.	Air Ship	Feb. 20, 1900	643,975
Pickett, H.	Scaffold	June 30, 1874	152,511
Pinn, T. B.	File Holder	Aug. 17, 1880	231,355
Polk, A. J.	Bicycle Support	Apr. 14, 1896	558,103
Pugsley, A.	Blind Stop	July 29, 1890	433,306
Purdy & Peters	Design for Spoons	Apr. 23, 1895	24,228
Purdy & Sadgwar	Folding Chair	June 11, 1889	405,117
Purdy, W.	Device for Sharpening Edged Tools	Oct. 27, 1896	570,337
Purdy, W.	Design for Sharpening Edged Tools	Aug. 16, 1898	609,367
Purdy, W.	Device for Sharpening Edged Tools	Aug. 1, 1899	630,106
Purvis, W. B.	Bag Fastener	Apr. 25, 1882	256,856
Purvis, W. B.	Hand Stamp	Feb. 27, 1883	273,149
Purvis, W. B.	Fountain Pen	Jan. 7, 1890	419,065
Purvis, W. B.	Electric Railway	May 1, 1894	519,291
Purvis, W. B.	Magnetic Car Balancing Device	May 21, 1895	539,542
Purvis, W. B.	Electric Railway Switch	Aug. 17, 1897	588,176
(Purvis also patented ten paper bag machines between 1884 and 1894.)			
Queen, W.	Guard for Companion Ways and Hatches	Aug. 18, 1891	458,131
Ray, E. P.	Chair Supporting Device	Feb. 21, 1899	620,078
Ray, L. P.	Dust Pan	Aug. 3, 1897	587,607
Reed, J. W.	Dough Kneader and Roller	Sep. 23, 1884	305,474
Reynolds, H. H.	Window Ventilator for Railroad Cars	Apr. 3, 1883	275,271
Reynolds, H. H.	Safety Gate for Bridges	Oct. 7, 1890	437,937
Reynolds, R. R.	Non-Refillable Bottle	May 2, 1899	624,092
Rhodes, J. B.	Water Closets	Dec. 19, 1899	639,290
Richardson, A. C.	Hame Fastener	Mar. 14, 1882	255,022
Richardson, A. C.	Churn	Feb. 17, 1891	446,470
Richardson, A. C.	Casket Lowering Device	Nov. 13, 1894	529,311
Richardson, A. C.	Insect Destroyer	Feb. 28, 1899	620,362
Richardson, A. C.	Bottle	Dec. 12, 1899	638,811
Richardson, W. H.	Cotton Chopper	June 1, 1886	343,140
Richardson, W. H.	Child's Carriage	June 18, 1889	405,599
Richardson, W. H.	Child's Carriage	June 18, 1889	405,600
Richey, C. V.	Car Coupling	June 15, 1897	584,650
Richey, C. V.	Railroad Switch	Aug. 3, 1897	587,657
Richey, C. V.	Railroad Switch	Oct. 26, 1897	592,448
Richey, C. V.	Fire Escape Bracket	Dec. 28, 1897	596,427
Richey, C. V.	Combined Hammock and Stretcher	Dec. 13, 1898	615,907
Rickman, A. L.	Overshoe	Feb. 8, 1898	598,816
Ricks, J.	Horseshoe	Mar. 30, 1886	338,781
Ricks, J.	Overshoes for Horses	June 6, 1899	626,245
Rillieux, N.	Sugar Refiner (Evaporating Pan)	Dec. 10, 1846	4,879
Robinson, E. R.	Casting Composite	Nov, 23, 1897	594,286
Robinson, E. R.	Electric Railway Trolley	Sep. 19, 1893	505,370
Robinson, J. H.	Life Saving Guards for Locomotives	Mar. 14, 1899	621,143
Robinson, J. H.	Life Saving Guards for Street Cars	Apr. 25, 1899	623,929
Robinson, J.	Dinner Pail	Feb. 1, 1887	356,852
Romain, A.	Passenger Register	Apr. 23, 1889	402,035
Ross, A. L.	Runner for Stops	Aug. 4, 1896	565,301
Ross, A. L.	Bag Closure	June 7, 1898	605,343
Ross, A. L.	Trousers Support	Nov. 28, 1899	638,068
Ross, J.	Bailing Press	Sep. 5, 1899	632,539

Roster, D. N.	Feather Curler	Mar. 10, 1896	556,166
Ruffin, S.	Vessels for Liquids and Manner of Sealing	Nov. 20, 1899	737,603
Russell, L. A.	Guard Attachment for Beds	Aug. 13, 1895	544,381
Sampson, G. T.	Sled Propeller	Feb. 17, 1885	312,388
Sampson, G. T.	Clothes Drier	June 7, 1892	476,416
Scottron, S. R.	Adjustable Window Cornice	Feb. 17, 1880	224,732
Scottron, S. R.	Cornice	Jan. 16, 1883	270,851
Scottron, S. R.	Pole Tip	Sep. 31, 1886	349,525
Scottron, S. R.	Curtain Rod	Aug. 30, 1892	481,720
Scottron, S. R.	Supporting Bracket	Sep. 12, 1893	505,008
Shanks, S. C.	Sleeping Car Berth Register	July 21, 1897	587,165
Shewcraft, F.	Letter Box	Detroit, Michigan	
Shorter, D. W.	Feed Rack	May 17, 1887	363,089
Smith, J. W.	Improvement in Games	Apr. 17, 1900	647,887
Smith, J. W.	Lawn Sprinkler	May 4, 1897	581,785
Smith, J. W.	Lawn Sprinkler	Mar. 22, 1898	601,065
Smith, P. D.	Potato Digger	Jan. 21, 1891	445,206
Smith, P. D.	Grain Binder	Feb. 23, 1892	469,279
Snow & Johns	Linament	Oct. 7, 1890	437,728
Spears, H.	Portable Shield for Infantry	Dec. 27, 1870	110,599
Spikes, R. B.	Combination Milk Bottle Opener & Bottle Cover	June 29, 1926	1,590,557
Spikes, R. B.	Method and Apparatus for Obtaining Average Samples and Temperature of Tank Liquids	Oct. 27, 1931	1,828,753
Spikes, R. B.	Automatic Gear Shift	Dec. 6, 1932	1,889,814
Spikes, R. B.	Transmission and Shifting Thereof	Nov. 28, 1933	1,936,996
Spikes, R. B.	Self-Locking Rack for Billiard Cues	around 1910	not found
Spikes, R. B.	Automatic Shoe Shine Chair	around 1939	not found
Spikes, R. B.	Multiple Barrel Machine Gun	around 1940	not found

(Some patents are not included here because of litigation; or because they were so basic in nature that redesigning and refiling procedures are now in process.)

Standard, J.	Oil Stove	Oct. 29, 1889	413,689
Standard, J.	Refrigerator	July 14, 1891	455,891
Stewart & Johnson	Metal Bending Machine	Dec. 27, 1887	375,512
Stewart, E. W.	Punching Machine	May 3, 1887	362,190
Stewart, E. W.	Machine for Forming Vehicle Sear Bars	Mar. 22, 1887	373,698
Stewart, T. W.	Mop	June 13, 1893	499,402
Stewart, T. W.	Station Indicator	June 20, 1893	499,895
Sutton, E. H.	Cotton Cultivator	Apr. 7, 1874	149,543
Sweeting, J. A.	Device for Rolling Cigarettes	Nov. 30, 1897	594,501
Sweeting, J. A.	Combined Knife and Scoop	June 7, 1898	605,209
Taylor, B. H.	Rotary Engine	Apr. 23, 1878	202,888
Taylor, B. H.	Slide Valve	July 6, 1897	585,798
Temple, L.	Toggle Harpoon	1848, "Eyewitness, Black History"	
Thomas, S. E.	Waste Trap	Oct. 16, 1883	286,746
Thomas, S. E.	Waste Trap for Basins, Closets, Etc.	Oct. 4, 1887	371,107
Thomas, S. E.	Casting	July 31, 1888	386,941
Thomas, S. E.	Pipe Connection	Oct. 9, 1888	390,821
Toliver, G.	Propeller for Vessels	Apr. 28, 1891	451,086
Tregoning & Latimer	Globe Supporter for Electric Lamps	Mar. 21, 1882	255,212
Walker, P.	Machine for Cleaning Seed Cotton	Feb. 16, 1897	577,153
Walker, P.	Bait Holder	Mar. 8, 1898	600,241
Waller, J. N.	Shoemaker's Cabinet or Bench	Feb. 3, 1880	224,253

Black Inventors of America

Washington, W.	Corn Husking Machine	Aug. 14, 1883	283,173
Watkins, Isaac	Scrubbing Frame	Oct. 7, 1890	437,849
Watts, J. R.	Bracket for Miners' Lamp	Mar. 7, 1893	493,137
West, E. H.	Weather Shield	Sep. 5, 1899	632,385
West, J. W.	Wagon	Oct. 18, 1870	108,419
White, D. L.	Extension Steps for Cars	Jan. 12, 1897	574,969
White, J. T.	Lemon Squeezer	Dec. 8, 1896	572,849
Williams, C.	Canopy Frame	Feb. 2, 1892	468,280
Williams, J. P.	Pillow Sham Holder	Oct. 10, 1899	634,784
Winn, Frank	Direct Acting Steam Engine	Dec. 4, 1888	394,047
Winters, J. B.	Fire Escape Ladder	May 7, 1878	203,517
Winters, J. R.	Fire Escape Ladder	Apr. 8, 1879	214,224
Woods, G. T.	Steam Boiler Furnace	June 3, 1884	299,894
Woods, G. T.	Telephone Transmitter	Dec. 2, 1884	308,876
Woods, G. T.	Apparatus for Transmission of Messages by Electricity	Apr. 7, 1885	315,368
Woods, G. T.	Relay Instrument	June 7, 1887	364,619
Woods, G. T.	Polarized Relay	July 5, 1887	366,192
Woods, G. T.	Electro Mechanical Brake	Aug. 16, 1887	368,265
Woods, G. T.	Telephone System and Apparatus	Oct. 11, 1887	371,241
Woods, G. T.	Electro Magnetic Brake Apparatus	Oct. 18, 1887	371,655
Woods, G. T.	Railway Telegraphy	Nov. 15, 1887	373,383
Woods, G. T.	Induction Telegraph System	Nov. 29, 1887	373,915
Woods, G. T.	Overhead Conducting System for Electric Railway	May 29, 1888	383,844
Woods, G. T.	Electro-Motive Railway System	June 26, 1888	385,034
Woods, G. T.	Runnel Construction for Electric Railway	July 17, 1888	386,282
Woods, G. T.	Galvanic Battery	Aug. 14, 1888	387,839
Woods, G. T.	Railway Telegraphy	Aug. 28, 1888	388,803
Woods, G. T.	Automatic Safety Cut-Out for Electric Circuits	Jan 1, 1889	395,533
Woods, G. T.	Electric Railway System	Nov. 10, 1891	463,020
Woods, G. T.	Electric Railway Conduit	Nov. 21, 1893	509,065
Woods, G. T.	System of Electrical Distribution	Oct. 13, 1896	569,443
Woods, G. T.	Amusement Apparatus	Dec. 19, 1899	639,692
Woods, G. T.	Electric Railway	Jan. 29, 1901	667,110
Woods, G. T.	Electric Railway System	July 9, l901	678,086
Woods, G. T.	Regulating and Controlling Electrical Translating Devices	Sep. 3, 1901	681,768
Woods, G. T.	Electric Railway	Nov. 19, 1901	687,098
Woods, G. T.	Automatic Air Brake	June 10, 1902	701,981
Woods, G. T.	Electric Railway System	Jan. 13, 1903	718,183
Woods, G. T.	Electric Railway	May 26, 1903	729,481
Wormley, J.	Life Saving Apparatus	May 24, 1881	242,091

Bibliography and Suggested Readings

American Council of Learned Societies *A guide to Documents in the National Archives for Negro Studies.* Washington, D.C., 1947.

Arons, Stephen *Compelling Belief* McGraw-Hill, 1983

Begeman, Myron L. *Manufacturing Processes* Wiley, 1952.

Bennett, Jr., Lerone *Before the Mayflower* Johnson, 1962.

Collins, Marva & Tamarkin, Civia. *Marva Collins' Way* J. P. Tarcher Inc., 1982.

Cross, Theodore L *Black Capitalism* Atheneum, 1969.

Gilder, George *The Spirit of Enterprise* Simon and Schuster, 1984.

Herkimer, Herbert *The Engineer's Illustrated Thesaurus* Chemical Publishing Co., 1952.

Katz, William L *Eyewitness, The Negro in American History* Pitman, 1967; also, *Teachers Guide to American Negro History*

Ploski and Brown *The Negro Almanac* Bellwether, 1967.

Production Handbook Ronald Press, (any recent edition)

Rodriguez, Richard *Hunger of Memory* Godine, 1982.

Sowell, Thomas *Black Education - Myths and Tragedies* McKay, 1972.

Sowell, Thomas *Civil Rights: Rhetoric or Reality?* Morrow, 1984.

Sowell, Thomas *A Conflict of Visions* Morrow, 1987.

Sowell, Thomas *The Economics and Politics of Race Morrow, 1983.*

Sowell, Thomas *Ethnic America* Basic Books, 1981.

Sowell, Thomas *Markets and Minorities* Basic Books, 1981.

Williams, Walter *The State Against Blacks* McGraw-Hill, 1982.

The foremost authority in the field is Dr. John Hope Franklin, writer of the LIFE Magazine series on Black history. Professor Franklin, a black, is Chairman of the University of Chicago History Department; and also Chairman of the Fulbright Board. A Harvard Ph.D. and formerly Pitt professor of American history at Cambridge, his material may be considered as fundamental to any integrated structuring of the "Black Scene."